# Corporate Social Responsibility Reporting in China

T0270820

In recent years, Corporate Social Responsibility (CSR) reporting in China has been developing rapidly, and the number of social reports issued by Chinese enterprises continues to sharply increase. This book investigates the evolution of this reporting practice in the country and the reasons behind it. In addition, it examines the reporting quantity and quality of Chinese enterprises by applying the GRI (Global Reporting Initiative) as an evaluation tool.

In order to obtain government recognition and receive more resources, state-owned enterprises, private enterprises, and foreign-invested companies have made substantial efforts in social reporting in terms of quantity and coverage. However, it appears that there is still room for enhancing the quality of disclosure. The book also highlights the central government's economic, political, and social roles in promoting, encouraging, and controlling the development of CSR reporting.

**Jieqi Guan** is Lecturer at Tourism College at the Institute for Tourism Studies, Macau.

**Carlos Noronha** is Associate Professor at the Faculty of Business Administration at the University of Macau.

# Routledge Contemporary China

For our full list of available titles:
www.routledge.com/Routledge-Contemporary-China-Series/book-series/SE0768

174 **Interest Groups and New Democracy Movement in Hong Kong**
*Edited by Sonny Shiu-Hing Lo*

175 **Civil Society in China and Taiwan**
Agency, Class and Boundaries
*Taru Salmenkari*

176 **Chinese Fans of Japanese and Korean Pop Culture**
Nationalistic Narratives and International Fandom
*Lu Chen*

177 **Emerging Adulthood in Hong Kong**
Social Forces and Civic Engagement
*Chau-kiu Cheung*

178 **Citizenship, Identity and Social Movements in the New Hong Kong**
Localism after the Umbrella Movement
*Edited by Wai Man Lam and Luke Cooper*

179 **The Politics of Memory in Sinophone Cinemas and Image Culture**
Altering Archives
*Edited by Peng Hsiao-yen and Ella Raidel*

180 **China's Soviet Dream**
Propaganda, Culture, and Popular Imagination
*Yan Li*

181 **Deng Xiaoping and China's Foreign Policy**
*Ronald C. Keith*

182 **Corporate Social Responsibility Reporting in China**
Evolution, Drivers and Prospects
*Jieqi Guan and Carlos Noronha*

# Corporate Social Responsibility Reporting in China

Evolution, Drivers and Prospects

Jieqi Guan and Carlos Noronha

LONDON AND NEW YORK

First published 2018 by Routledge

2 Park Square, Milton Park, Abingdon, Oxfordshire OX14 4RN
52 Vanderbilt Avenue, New York, NY 10017

*Routledge is an imprint of the Taylor & Francis Group, an informa business*

First issued in paperback 2019

*British Library Cataloguing-in-Publication Data*
A catalogue record for this book is available from the British Library

*Library of Congress Cataloging-in-Publication Data*
Names: Guan, Jieqi, author. | Noronha, Carlos, author.
Title: Corporate social responsibility reporting in China : evolution,
    drivers and prospects / by Jieqi Guan and Carlos Noronha.
Description: 1 Edition. | New York : Routledge, 2018. | Series: Routledge
    contemporary China series ; 182 | Includes bibliographical references
    and index.
Identifiers: LCCN 2017033618 | ISBN 9780415787871 (hardback) |
    ISBN 9781315225685 (ebook)
Subjects: LCSH: Social responsibility of business—China. | Social
    accounting—China.
Classification: LCC HD60.5.C6 G83 2017 | DDC 338.70951—dc23
LC record available at https://lccn.loc.gov/2017033618

ISBN: 978-0-415-78787-1 (hbk)
ISBN: 978-0-367-37476-1 (pbk)

Typeset in Goudy
by Apex CoVantage, LLC

# Contents

*List of figures* vii
*List of tables* viii
*Foreword* ix
*Acknowledgments* xii
*Abbreviations* xiii

1 Introduction 1

2 Literature review and theoretical framework 10

3 Institutional environment and legal system of CSR 20

4 CSR reporting of state-owned enterprises: an overall perspective 30

5 CSR reporting of state-owned enterprises: some specifics and reporting trends 44

6 The social roles of private enterprises 51

7 CSR reporting of private companies 61

8 Development of foreign-invested companies in China 70

9 CSR reporting of foreign-invested companies in China 79

10 Triangulation: empirical study and interview analysis 87

11 Further discussion and conclusions 98

*References* 107
*Appendix 1: summary of 2011 scandals in China* 119
*Appendix 2: summary of key mandatory and voluntary*
  *standards/guidelines on CSR reporting issues in China* 124
*Appendix 3: GRI framework* 128
*Appendix 4: coverage of CSR dimensions for largest SOEs in*
  *China from 210 annual reports and 117 social reports* 129
*Appendix 5: statistics of content analysis results* 130
*Appendix 6: disclosure of bad news and industrial accidents* 132
*Appendix 7: ranking of CSR reporting by industries* 133
*Appendix 8: statistics on foreign direct investments* 134
*Index* 135

# Figures

1.1    Structure of the research    6
2.1    The development of SAR theories    13
3.1    The structure of institutional environment in China    21
4.1    Number of CSR reports issued by listed enterprises in China    33
4.2    Average coverage of CSR dimensions in 210 annual reports of the largest SOEs in China    38
4.3    Number of CSR key words disclosed in 210 annual reports of the largest SOEs in China    39
4.4    Number of CSR key words disclosed in 210 annual reports of the largest SOEs in China by indicators    39
4.5    Average coverage of CSR dimensions in 117 social reports of the largest SOEs in China    40
4.6    Overall quality of CSR disclosure in the largest SOEs in China from 210 annual reports and 117 social reports    41
4.7    Average quality of CSR disclosure in the largest SOEs in China from 210 annual reports and 117 social reports    41
5.1    Ranking of CSR reporting by industries    46
5.2    Chronological sketch of social reporting development in China    47
7.1    Number of CSR key words disclosed in annual reports    63
7.2    Number of CSR key words disclosed in social reports    63
7.3    Quality of CSR disclosure in annual reports    64
7.4    Quality of CSR disclosure in social reports    65
7.5    Analysis of CSR disclosure on websites    67
9.1    Number of CSR key words in annual reports    81
9.2    Number of CSR key words in social reports    82
9.3    Quality of CSR disclosure in annual reports    84
9.4    Quality of CSR disclosure in social reports    84
11.1    Top-down model    99
11.2    Bottom-up model    102
11.3    CSR reporting drivers of SOEs in China    103
11.4    CSR reporting framework of private firms and MNCs    103

# Tables

| | | |
|---|---|---|
| 3.1 | Summary of laws with CSR ingredients | 23 |
| 4.1 | Distribution of SOEs' annual reports and social reports selected | 35 |
| 4.2 | Summary of CSR dimensions | 36 |
| 5.1 | Comparison of coverage in CSR dimensions between SOEs in high-profile and low-profile industries in China | 45 |
| 7.1 | Distribution of private enterprises, annual reports, and social reports | 62 |
| 8.1 | Foreign investments in high-tech industry | 75 |
| 8.2 | Weight of foreign direct investment (FDI) in the national economy | 76 |
| 8.3 | Import and export of foreign-invested companies (% billion US dollars) | 77 |
| 9.1 | Distribution of foreign enterprises (MNCs), annual reports, and social reports | 80 |
| 10.1 | Descriptive statistics of variables with main interest | 91 |
| 10.2 | Correlation matrix of variables with main interest | 91 |
| 10.3 | Regression results | 92 |
| 10.4 | Sample distribution of interviews | 94 |
| 10.5 | Interview guide | 94 |
| 10.6 | Motivation to report social information | 95 |

# Foreword

It is a pleasure to write the foreword to this work, *Corporate Social Responsibility Reporting in China: Evolution, drivers and prospects* by Jieqi "Jenny" Guan and Carlos Noronha. I was made aware of their research into Corporate Social Responsibility (CSR) on the occasions of my visits to the University of Macau when engaged on other projects. We had various discussions about Chinese CSR, and during this time I learned more about the nature of Chinese businesses, their environment, and Social Accounting and Reporting (SAR) in China.

The significant growth and impact of China in recent decades can hardly have escaped the notice of anyone with even a slight interest in business or the world economy. It has been observed that a quarter of all the cranes in the world were once operating in China, and further, that the Chinese middle class was growing at a rate equaling the size of a medium city every month. Alongside this economic development of China there was evidence of the impact of that development on the environment and society, including increased pollution and concern over health and safety issues as well as issues related to economic growth and sustainability. Press stories of health scares and scandals occurred in both the Chinese and world media.

Hence there were calls for the Chinese government and Chinese companies to report, "to account for," their social and environmental impacts. It is against this background that Jenny Guan and Carlos Noronha have produced this monograph. It presents significant factual empirical detail charting the emergence of CSR reporting in China beginning with the first CSR report in 2006, and thus makes documentation of CSR reporting in the Chinese language more accessible internationally.

The work contains a number of aspects. Following their introduction and background, they briefly discuss political economy theory (PET), legitimacy theory (LT), and stakeholder theory (ST), frameworks that are widely used in international CSR journal articles explaining social accountability. In addition, they cover the Chinese institutional and legal environment, for example, government regulations, instructions, and "incentives" both formal and informal, to fulfil Social Accounting and Reporting (SAR). They make reference to and speculate on the role played by the consumer, the public image and reputation, and the media in informing society or setting an agenda in relation to the SAR process.

Content analysis of corporate reports and sustainability reports features prominently in their empirical reporting. In other words, Jenny and Carlos are answering the question, "What is currently being reported?" This is delivered in separate chapters related to state-owned enterprises (SOEs), private companies (PCs) and multinational companies (MNCs) in which the data is presented, explained, and analyzed. Preceding each of the above are chapters explaining the development and prevailing environment of each of these business types. For example, contrary to what the name suggests, SOEs do have some private ownership. PCs are currently the fastest-growing sector, while MNCs (which originated as joint ventures) are increasingly not only locating manufacturing to China but also introducing R&D there, thus contributing to changing the character of business. They also go into greater detail on some aspects in that they contrast high-profile and low-profile SOEs, demonstrating statistically that there is a significant difference in the content of the reporting by these businesses given their different risk profiles.

To structure their content, they use the Global Reporting Initiative (GRI) guidelines on CSR, which offer benefits in terms of potential for comparability with international work by other authors and in developing future research. All the detail of CSR content is supported by tables and charts showing the extent of disclosure in different dimensions of the GRI requirements, a word (or Chinese character) count, and assessment of the quality of reporting. Quality refers to the extent of explanation of the impact of CSR actions taken, including appropriate quantification, rather than just platitudes about desirable actions. They do not restrict themselves to factors occurring and being mentioned in corporate reports and CSR reports and websites. In the research, they undertook cross references to social media and press commentary. They are thus able to reveal where a scandal occurred and if the companies concerned made any reference to their role in the scandal and to the steps taken to ensure such an event did not recur.

Their results reveal a growth over time (2006–2010) in disclosure quantity, but perhaps not a comparable improvement in quality. They comment on various dysfunctionalities that are observed in the system, revealing potential or actual conflicts of interest and factors that may be encouraging inappropriate practices and over which academics and the media can play a role in revealing.

They undertake regression analyses to support their propositions, applied to a different and larger data set, extracted from the Shanghai Stock Exchange (2008–2013). They conclude that firms with greater political relations and those with greater links to local and industrial associations perform better in CSR reporting. Additionally, companies that experienced greater media attention also present better-quality CSR reports, and finally, SOEs outperform private companies in the quality of their CSR disclosures.

They also report the results of semi-structured interviews to obtain the opinions of influential executives and others related to the publication of SARs. In summary, this revealed that the most important reasons for Chinese CSR disclosures were those of government policies and legal obligations, while much less importance was given to satisfying the concerns of society generally, following others in the industry (isomorphism), or to increase profit. Finally, they map out a tentative model with particular reference to SOEs, which they believe has a bearing on the CSR reporting in China in what they describe as a top-down/bottom-up model.

Jenny and Carlos have produced a very important reader on the emergence of CSR reporting in China, the drivers of it, and the background in which it is taking place. It is extremely comprehensive, not just in the CSR reporting but in description and explanation of the Chinese environment, the literature review, and hence as a basis for other researchers' investigations. It is a worthy read for those with interest in Chinese business generally or CSR in particular.

Professor Mike Tayles
Emeritus Professor of Accounting and Finance
Hull University Business School
University of Hull

# Acknowledgments

We would like to take this opportunity to thank all those individuals who have helped us in the preparation of this book. We are grateful for the academic support of Professors Mary Chai, Teresa Chu, Philip Law, Jacky So, Desmond Yuen, and Steven Zhang. In particular, we wish to express our sincerest gratitude to Professor Michael Tayles for providing us with his supportive and constructive advice throughout the process during his periodic visits to the University of Macau. Thanks are also due to the staff at Routledge, especially Yongling Lam and Samantha Phua, as well as the anonymous reviewers who helped to make this project possible.

In addition, we would like to thank the Research and Development Administration Office of the University of Macau for providing us funding on various phases of this study.

Last but not least, we would like to thank all the research assistants and friends who have supported us in all possible ways.

J.G.
C.N.

# Abbreviations

| | |
|---|---|
| ASSO | association relation |
| BODSIZE | board size |
| BPE | bourgeois political economy |
| BRICs | Brazil, Russia, India and China |
| CAITEC | Chinese Academy of International Trade and Economic Cooperation |
| CASC | China Accounting Standards Committee |
| CBIA | China Banking Industry Association |
| CBRC | China Banking Regulatory Commission |
| CCP | Chinese Communist Party |
| CFCE | Chinese-foreign cooperative enterprises |
| CFIE | China Federation of Industrial Economics |
| CICPMC | China International Council for the Promotion of Multi-national Corporations |
| CNTAC | China National Textile and Apparel Council |
| CON | ownership concentration |
| CPE | classical political economy |
| CPPCC | Chinese People's Political Consultative Conference |
| CSR | corporate social responsibility |
| CSRC | China Securities Regulatory Commission |
| EC | economic |
| EHS | environment, health, and safety |
| EN | environment |
| GCE | governance, commitments and engagement |
| GLCs | government-linked companies |
| GRI | Global Reporting Initiative |
| IND | industry |
| LA | labor practices and decent work |
| LEV | leverage |
| LT | legitimacy theory |
| MED | media attention |
| MFPRC | Ministry of Finance of the People's Republic of China |
| MNEs | multinational enterprises |
| NCCPC | National Congresses of the Communist Party of China |

| NPC | National People's Congress |
| OP | organizational profile |
| PET | political economy theory |
| POL | political relation |
| PR | product responsibility |
| RP | report parameters |
| SA | strategy and analysis |
| SAR | social accounting and reporting |
| SASAC | State-owned Assets Supervision and Administration Commission |
| SCPRC | State Council of the PRC |
| SEPA | State Environmental Protection Administration |
| SFEJV | Sino-foreign equity joint venture |
| SGCC | State Grid Corporation of China |
| SIZE | company size |
| SO | society |
| SOEs | state-owned enterprises |
| SR | social report |
| SSE | Shanghai Stock Exchange |
| ST | stakeholder theory |
| SZSE | Shenzhen Stock Exchange |
| WFOE | wholly foreign-owned enterprises |

# 1 Introduction

## General background

Corporate social responsibility (CSR) reporting has become a very important tool that helps enterprises to implement strategies and build their core competencies. Through social reporting, firms are able to tell the public what socially desirable actions they have taken. A majority of the Fortune 1000 firms publish social reports regularly (Jo and Kim, 2008). This behavior helps a corporation to make a good impression on their stakeholders and on society as a whole (Shin, 2014).

CSR can be interpreted as the actions taken voluntarily by public companies that contribute to building a better society and cleaner environment. During this process, they consider the social and environmental impacts during their business operations and communicate the related issues to stakeholders. However, if companies wish to tell the public what they have done and what they have failed to do, a medium for communication is needed. For this reason, social accounting and reporting (SAR) was introduced. It is an effective way to express the accountability of a business to particular interest groups and to describe the social and environmental impacts of the enterprise's operating activities (Gray, 2001). SAR has attracted considerable research interest since the 1980s and has played an increasingly significant role in different societies and countries where better living standards have been achieved (Tsang, 1996). Gray et al. defined corporate social reporting as "the process of communicating the social and environmental effects of organizations' economic actions to particular interest groups within society and to society at large" (Gray et al., 1987, p. ix). In the past decades, the CSR movement has spread geographically from the Western world, its area of origin, to Asia, particularly in developing countries. Given the considerable variations in the economic, cultural, and legal environments, the practices of SAR in developing countries have significant differences from those in the developed world (Belal, 2008). In developing countries, CSR is being emphasized more for its philanthropic aspects, since many Asians practice Hinduism, Buddhism, Islam, and Christianity (Visser, 2008). The specific social and economic environment also plays a particular role. For example, in Nigeria, social reporting is specifically aimed at addressing the socioeconomic development of the country, mainly in the areas of access to health care, poverty alleviation, establishment of education, and infrastructure development (Amaeshi et al., 2006). This is in contrast to many Western countries, where CSR is prioritized on climate change concerns, fair trade, consumer protection, green marketing, or socially responsible investments (Schmidheiny, 2006; De Oliveira, 2006; Amaeshi et al., 2006). As indicated by Belal (2008), "CSR reporting is yet to develop significantly in developing countries which could be due to lack of regulation and also due to lack of influence from the pressure groups . . . However, . . . more and more companies in developing countries around the world are coming forward with significant social and environmental reports." Therefore, this creates an opportunity for extending SAR research in developing countries.

## Specific background

Among these developing countries, China stands out. After more than three decades of reform, opening up, and rapid growth, China became the world's second-largest economy in 2010.[1] Recent development has attracted worldwide attention, as the country progresses along the journey from a planned economy to a market economy. The transition is not yet complete. At its current stage of development, China is facing a major challenge. That is to say, the question of how to balance between economic growth and sustainability. Evidence of this challenge has been shown in the adverse publicity related to some industrial and commercial operations, including environmental pollution, resource utilization, product quality, and labor protection problems.

In China, there has been an increasing number of firms causing significant negative impact on society. For instance, in 2008 the San Lu Corporation produced poisoned milk powder that led to the death of at least six infants and resulted in more than 300,000 sick children in China.[2] This scandal caused consumers to lose confidence in the Chinese milk powder industry (Noronha and Kong, 2015). Foxconn, the world's largest contract electronics manufacturer, located in Shenzhen, saw 18 of its young workers commit suicide in 2010[3] (Noronha and Wang, 2015). In the following year, an illegal additive, clenbuterol, was found in the products of China's largest meat processor, Shuanghui Group,[4] leading Chinese consumers to lose faith in the food-processing giant. The above are just selected examples. Many other serious industrial scandals were disclosed in the *2011 Multinationals' CSR Problem Report* issued by the China International Council for the Promotion of Multinational Corporations (CICPMC) (see Appendix 1). For instance, Carrefour and Walmart stores in China were caught using illegal pricing methods such as stating fake original prices when advertising sale items. Mengniu Dairy was exposed by the mass media about the quality issues of tainted milk several times. China Datang Corporation, one of the largest power supply enterprises was penalized for excessive discharge of sulfur dioxide at more than 60 percent and for environmental pollution. All these companies mentioned in the report play leading roles in their own industries, and most of them are members of the Fortune 500 (MCSRR, 2011).

These scandals have caused serious criticisms and revealed the lack of social responsibility awareness within Chinese enterprises. In recent years, a growing number of Chinese firms have started to conduct CSR activities in order to distinguish themselves from scandals and to build a good business image. To inform the public what socially responsible actions they have taken, more and more companies produce CSR reports and use them as an important way to communicate their social contributions to stakeholders. According to the statistics of the *China WTO Tribune*, the number of CSR reports published in 2011 increased by almost 10 percent compared with those in 2010 (531 in 2011 vs. 483 in 2010). The rate is up to 43 percent if comparing with 2009's figure (531 in 2011 vs. 371 in 2009). This demonstrates that there has been a growing awareness of social reporting within Chinese enterprises. Barnett (2007) and Mackey et al., (2007) pointed out that many companies that engage in CSR are mainly motivated by the contribution to the company's financial performance or on the firm's market value. To avoid damaging a company's brand image or business reputation, many Chinese enterprises only disclose good CSR performance in their reports and draw a veil over scandals or bad news. Take two of the abovementioned scandals as examples. San Lu failed to disclose its milk source in the 2008 annual and CSR reports and even avoided the reporting of the milk powder scandal in its subsequent public reports. In Shuanghui Group's 2011 reports, no information about the food-processing additives and supply chain was disclosed. Similarly, San Lu made no mention of the illegal additive scandal in its reports. It was as if nothing had happened at all.

Therefore, to inspire and help more enterprises prepare and issue high-quality CSR reports, and to facilitate the healthy development of China's SAR, the government and many regulatory bodies have given prominence to this issue and have promulgated a series of policies and documents to provide incentives and support for SAR development (see Appendix 2). From one perspective, CSR advocates are glad to see the increasing number of CSR initiatives appearing in China. From another perspective, those advocates may also question the effectiveness of these initiatives. How sincere and serious are the Chinese SAR measures? Is SAR in China simply window dressing, or is there any real structural change underway? These questions arise because it appears that enterprises keep producing "clean" and "green" reports while one scandal still follows hard on another.

This situation may be due to the fact that China's market economy is centrally controlled by the government, which manages personnel selection and evaluation, market channels, and resource allocation, especially in state-owned enterprises (SOEs) (Lin, 2011). Voluntary CSR reporting acts as responses to institutional forces from the central/local government and market-based institutions in transitional markets (Lin, 2010). Therefore, studying SAR not only can provide an important way to understand the CSR performance of public enterprises (Ullmann, 1985; Magness, 2006) but can also evaluate the quality and transparency of the issued reports.

**Research problem and objectives**

Currently there is no unified social reporting guideline for public companies in China, and external assurance on non-financial reporting is not mandatory. Therefore, the credibility of social accounting information disclosed is difficult for stakeholders to assess. Indeed, "currently, there is almost no published research in English accounting journals on mainland Chinese CSR reporting . . . it is proposed that more research is undertaken on the development of CSR reporting in the BRICs (Brazil, Russia, India and China) countries" (Belal, 2008, p. 142). In July 2011, an English CSR reporting study about China was undertaken by Kuo et al. They evaluated the quality of social disclosure in CSR reports by applying content analysis. A small number of other papers discussed CSR in China and made comparisons with other countries. However, most of them were anecdotal since they did not have empirical data or were not China-specific. Therefore, the lack of studies in CSR aspects becomes the core of the problem and thus more empirical research on SAR in China is urgently called for.

China is in a transitional stage from a planned economy to a market economy. During this period, many enterprises choose to use political network strategies for accessing more resources. This is mainly due to the fact that the transition is likely to have some kind of weaknesses, such as uneven distribution of resources, low work efficiency due to the incomplete integration of planned economy and market economy (Fan et al., 2007). Additionally, China depends on a one-party political system governed by the Chinese Communist Party (CCP). "Harmonious society" (*hexie shehui*) is a core concept initiated by President Hu Jintao in 2002. This concept is treated as a goal for future socioeconomic development in the country (Lam, 2005). The concept was also integrated into the 11th Five-Year Plan (2006–2010)[5] announced by the government and was added into the constitution of the CCP.[6] Considering the importance of the relationship between government and enterprises in China, especially in the building of a harmonious society and the adjustment of the economic structure and the improvement of the CSR environment, the question of "whether political pressures or factors drive enterprises to conduct CSR activities and reporting in China?" is worth studying. It is suggested that CSR needs to be analyzed critically in the context of a fundamental shift in political power among state, market, and civil society actors (Fuchs, 2007; Hirschland, 2006; Moon and Vogel, 2008). However, the extant researches mainly focus on some other areas rather than CSR, such as political influence on technological innovation and investment strategies (Hillman et al., 2004). Thus, the political impact on CSR reporting of companies in transitional economies leaves much to be investigated.

This study aims at ascertaining empirically the social reporting practices in mainland China by conducting content analyses of companies' annual and CSR reports and interview records so as to generate hypotheses to investigate the driving forces behind the SAR. The primary objective is to develop a model or theoretical framework of SAR that reflects the uniqueness of China, the largest emerging economy. To achieve this, it is very important to understand what lies between the existing SAR theories (e.g., political economy theory, legitimacy theory, stakeholder theory) and the Chinese CSR environment. Then, some of these existing theories are applied into the context of China's unique institutional characteristics to attempt to develop a theory based on those unique features. This leads to our major research question.

What is (are) the SAR framework(s) for enterprises in China and what is (are) the force(s) that drive Chinese enterprises to address their SAR performance?

In order to tackle these questions, the following steps are taken:

1  Trace the history of the emergence of CSR disclosure among Chinese enterprises;
2  Understand the institutional environment and practice of CSR reporting in China;
3  Assess the level and extent of social disclosure in annual reports, CSR reports, and official websites of different types of enterprises in China;
4  Investigate the patterns (e.g., category, item, focus, amount, and difference per category) of companies in practicing social disclosure;
5  Verify the reliability and transparency of social information disclosed in the annual reports and CSR reports;
6  Explore management's perceptions and motivations behind the social disclosure in the annual reports and CSR reports of different types of enterprises in China.

## Research design

Figure 1.1 presents the main structure of this research. First, a broad literature review is performed to obtain a thorough understanding of theories of SAR by reviewing empirical researches in the Western and Chinese academia, the international initiatives, and the legal and regulatory systems of SAR in China. Second, for Chinese enterprises, comprehensive content analyses of annual reports, CSR reports, and official websites are conducted. The results are then associated with the findings from interviews conducted at a later stage. Finally, the outcome of the study is reconciled with the theories and literature. Any discrepancies are further investigated and analyzed. The application of mixed methods as triangulation is a powerful technique that facilitates "validation of data through cross verification from more than two sources" (Bogdan and Biklen, 2006, p. 114). The primary goal is to apply and combine content analyses and interviews in studying the SAR phenomenon in China.

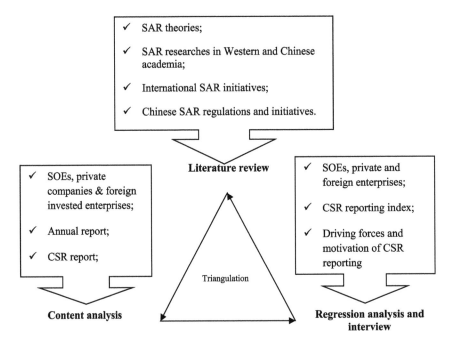

*Figure 1.1* Structure of the research

## Research methodology

### Content analysis

Content analysis of annual reports, CSR reports, sustainability reports and companies' official websites is the major data collection and analysis method in this research. Content analysis has been used quite widely in CSR research to capture the key elements of "communicated material through classification, tabulation, and evaluation of its key symbols and themes in order to ascertain its meaning and probable effect" (Unerman, 2000, p. 671). Content analysis has been used in empirical CSR studies by a number of scholars (see, for example, Guthrie and Parker, 1990, Adams and Harte, 1999; Perrini, 2006; Mirfazli, 2008).

In this study, both quantitative and qualitative approaches are applied. On the one hand, words, sentences, figures, and numbers in the reports related to the disclosure of CSR information are coded and recorded for statistical purposes. On the other hand, those words and sentences are further analyzed and reviewed to identify their underlying meanings. In this way, managers' perceptions, intentions, or motivations behind the disclosure of CSR information can be explored.

For selecting samples in this research, firms in China are classified into three groups, because different types of enterprises have different characteristics and specific responsibilities. First, state-owned enterprises (SOEs), as the mainstay of China's economy, reflect the country's development strategy by striving to set an example for CSR performance. Second, foreign-invested (multinational) companies, as direct beneficiaries of China's reform and opening up policy and important contributors to the Chinese economy, take CSR performance as an integral part of corporate localization. Third, private enterprises are one of the most active sections of the Chinese economy and practice social responsibility in order to embrace international competition.

A combined stratified and cluster sampling selection method is adopted. A total of 782 reports of 182 companies from the three abovementioned groups are selected for the period of 2006–2010, covering 14 industry sectors categorized by the China Securities Regulatory Commission. After processing the collected data, the results are analyzed in terms of industry sectors and ownership types. Due to the unique institutional and political environment in China, companies from different sectors or of different ownership types may behave differently in their social accounting practices. In addition, further investigation is made through interviews with various entities so as to identify the potential causes and consequences of the SAR phenomenon in China. By investigating the SAR characteristics in China, hopefully some new insights may be added on to existing CSR theories or that a new explanation can be developed to fit the unique situation in China or in other transitional and developing economies.

### Regression analysis

As mentioned earlier, it is believed that political pressures or factors drive enterprises to conduct CSR activities and reporting in China. Therefore, a regression model is constructed to investigate the relationship between political connections and the fulfillment of social reporting among Chinese listed enterprises and in turn to demonstrate whether firms with stronger political backgrounds or closer connections with the government perform differently in CSR reporting. Additionally, the regression results can be related back to the content analysis findings to see whether substantial differences exist and to serve as a reliability test for the overall research findings.

The analysis is based on data collected from public firms listed in the Shanghai and Shenzhen Stock Exchanges. The observation covers six consecutive years from 2008 to 2013 and 2,927 firm-year observations are generated from the CSMAR database. Beside political influence, this study also investigates the impact of media attention on firms' CSR performance and compares the CSR reporting level between SOEs and private enterprises. The results can further reinforce the content analysis findings as mentioned earlier.

### Interview

After completion of the quantitative content analysis, interviews or conference calls with public companies, academic institutions, NGOs, regulatory authorities, and business associations were arranged. The main purpose was to discuss the findings of our content analysis with industry representatives. Thus, their views of SAR, comments on this research, and ideas for further SAR development for Chinese enterprises can be collected.

The field work is carried out in the financial centers of North, East, South, and Central China, namely, Beijing, Shanghai, Guangzhou/Shenzhen, and Changsha. In all the cases, data are collected from semi-structured interviews (refer to Chapter 7 for details).

The content analysis and interview results are then "tied back" to the literature review described earlier, which provides a summary of the whole research and explains the SAR framework in China. Different research methods are used until a clear trend of social reporting can be determined. Finally, a new model is developed from the empirical research findings and content analysis and interview results.

## Research contributions

This is one of the first researches in Western academia to report, from an indigenous perspective, results of content analyses, empirical studies, and interview analyses of social reporting by Chinese enterprises so as to present the evolution of the practice in China. This is also the first research to add insight to the political economy theory and the interaction between political economy theory and legitimacy theory for explaining social reporting practices of the largest socialist and transitional economy in the world. Furthermore, the research can be replicated in other transitional economies for comparative studies in the future. Finally, we hope to help Chinese enterprises become aware of how they can improve the quality of their social reporting and provide guidance for their stakeholders to evaluate such social reports objectively.

## Overview of the remaining chapters

The remaining parts of the book are structured as follows.

Chapter 2 contains a comprehensive review dealing with SAR theories, literature, and initiatives and also includes a description and analysis of SAR development in Western and Chinese academia. Base on the literature review, research gaps are identified for SAR in China.

Chapter 3 introduces the institutional environment and legal system of CSR in China, which covers the administrative and governance system, the constitution, laws, and regulations. In addition, legislation on various stakeholder groups are also summarized.

Chapters 4 to 9 discuss the roles of the SOEs, private and foreign- invested (multinational) companies, in China and present methods and statistical results from content analysis of the reports for each type of enterprises. A comparison of social reporting practices is also conducted among enterprises within different industries.

Chapter 10 explains the methodologies, results, and findings of the regression and interview analyses, which are used as tools for triangulation and to demonstrate the robustness of the content analysis results.

Chapter 11 summarizes the findings from previous chapters. For any differences and conflicts identified, a new SAR framework is conceptualized that takes into consideration the specificities and uniqueness of the current situation in China. The chapter then wraps up the entire study and discusses the major findings. Contributions, limitations, and suggestions for future researches are stated as well.

## Notes

1 BBC News dated February 14, 2011, available at www.bbc.com/news/business-12427321
2 BBC News dated January 25, 2010, available at news.bbc.co.uk/2/hi/7720404.stm
3 CBS News dated August 7, 2013, available at www.cbsnews.com/news/what-happened-after-the-foxconn-suicides/
4 China Daily News dated March 16, 2011, available at www.chinadaily.com.cn/china/2011-03/16/content_12182955.htm
5 11th five-year plan is available at www.gov.cn/english/2006-03/07/content_246929.htm
6 Xinhua News dated October 25, 2007, available at news.xinhuanet.com/english/2007–2010/25/content_6944738.htm

# 2  Literature review and theoretical framework

## Researches in Western and Chinese academia

SAR initially appeared in the early 1970s when researches of reporting in relation to employees and products were conducted. In the 1980s, this topic was largely replaced by a growing number of studies about the "how" and the "impact" of accounting in reporting CSR information. In the late 1990s, environmental topics made a significant contribution to the social accounting literature (Aerts and Cormier, 2009; Cormier et al., 2005; Al-Tuwaijri et al., 2004; Bewley and Li, 2000). Discussions on environmental disclosures also appeared in many empirical studies during the same period (Gray et al., 1995; Hackston and Milne, 1996; Deegan and Rankin, 1996; Bebbington et al., 1999). In particular, the increasing number of studies in this topic has driven "the development of several frameworks and models to guide professionals in their approaches to environmental auditing and accounting" (Mathews, 1997, p. 496). A growing attention by the international community to CSR reporting began to appear at the start of the new millennium. Various issues such as those in relation to the dimensions and the levels of social disclosure and their determinants as well as managerial and stakeholder perceptions have been published (Belal and Momin, 2009). A number of them have investigated the evolution and achievements of SAR studies in developed countries through literature review (e.g., Alcañiz et al., 2010; Burritt and Schaltegger, 2010; Deegan and Soltys, 2007; Eugénio et al., 2010; Gray, 2002; Owen, 2008; Parker, 2005). However, there has been a lack of CSR information in developing countries, as the SAR literature mainly focuses on developed regions (Belal and Momin, 2009).

Belal and Momin (2009) have reviewed empirical social reporting researches of less-developed regions published in English accounting journals from the 1980s to the 2000s. More than 40 empirical studies were identified from over 10 countries across four regions. According to them, the majority of the researches focus on Asia Pacific, but none was related to mainland China, notwithstanding its being the strongest economy in the region. It was not until 2011 that research in English about CSR reporting in China was published (Kuo et al. (2011). They assessed the quality of social information disclosed in companies' social reports using content analysis. Nevertheless, the shortage of literature about China is still problematic to anyone wanting an overview of reporting in the region, since many Chinese CSR researches are mainly published domestically and it is questionable whether they are ready to be exposed to international academia.

The concept of CSR was brought to China in the early 1990s when a number of industrial scandals and accidents began to emerge (Guan and Noronha, 2013). For example, "the Gouhou dam burst disaster in Qinghai (1993); the explosion of dynamite stored in the basement of a five-story apartment building in Hunan (1996); the collapse of the under construction Baikong bridge in Shaoguan (1996) and the innumerable coal mine accidents" (Wikipedia, 2011). CSR studies in China began to develop, with the first monograph[1]being published in 1990 (Li and Liu, 2010). Since 2000, research in this field burgeoned. Government bodies, research institutions, and various social entities published conceptual papers on this topic. However, journal articles about CSR reporting started to appear only between 2010 and 2013.

Similar to most SAR researches in the West, social disclosure (Mobley, 1970; Beams and Fertig, 1971; Churchman, 1971; Mathew, 1993; Gray et al., 1997) as the predecessor of CSR reporting was studied by Chinese scholars before 2000 (Chen et al., 1998; Li and Jiang, 1998; Shan, 2000). However, these researchers only focused on the general analysis of some social problems and gave recommendations to encourage enterprises to do CSR reporting voluntarily. Since 2002, following the introduction of the Global Reporting Initiative (GRI) to China, scholars started to discuss the standardization of social accounting and disclosure (Han and Du, 2002; Zhang, 2002; Luo and Guan, 2003; Li, 2004; Zhang, 2004). However, the growing attention to SAR did not drive up additional research contributions. Most of the scholars provided armchair suggestions, and very few empirical researches were published during that period (Liu, 2003). There was a significant period of stagnation of SAR research in China.

After 2008, CSR studies in China focused more on the examination of CSR reporting (Huang et al., 2009; Deng and Chen, 2009; Fu and Zhu, 2010; Li, 2010; Wang, L., 2010; Zheng, 2010; Xia and Li, 2010; Yang and Chen, 2010; Lu and Li, 2010; Han and Ji, 2010; Jin and Zhu, 2010; Li and Peng, 2010). In addition, the impact of social disclosure on firms' performance and stakeholder reaction also became a popular topic (Cui, 2009; Yang, 2009; He and Hou, 2009; Li and Mu, 2010; Shi and Wang, 2010; An et al., 2010). In addition, the Bureau of Scientific Research of the Chinese Academy of Social Sciences published the *Blue Book of Corporate Social Responsibility* in 2009, 2010, and 2011, in which the social reporting level of the top 100 Chinese enterprises was assessed based on the information disclosed in their CSR reports, annual reports, and official websites. These three research reports have been treated as the official SAR research documents and stimulated a strong response from Chinese society. However, in the reports, only a self-developed indicator system instead of an internationally recognized CSR initiative was used for evaluating companies' performance. In addition, in 2009, when the first CSR report was published, it received a lot of criticism on the accuracy of the results and the research method. Therefore, more comprehensive SAR studies on Chinese enterprises employing sound CSR indicator systems such as the GRI and systematic research methodologies are warranted.

## Theoretical framework

The information disclosure system has close relationships with the establishment and development of capital markets (Campbell, 2007). The traditional financial statements are the sources of core information. However, the deficiency is that too much emphasis is being placed on shareholders and therefore other stakeholders' interests are overlooked, and this will probably make the company fail to achieve the goal of sustainable development. Nowadays, the company is not merely an "economic person" but a "social person" who lives in connection with society and multiple stakeholders. The traditional opinion that the company only accounts for financial reporting is out of accord with the times (Mousa, 2010; Campbell et al., 2006; Garriga and Mele, 2004). Therefore, it is necessary for the company to disclose social information to reflect its situation, plans, and corresponding measures of CSR.

At present, the CSR disclosure practice and the research on social reporting are still immature in China (Zhao et al., 2012). However, with the fast development of the country's economy, more and more enterprises have realized the importance of social responsibility and treat SAR as an effective way of communication with the public. In 2006, the State Grid Corporation of China (SGCC) issued their first CSR report, which was highly regarded by the Premier of the State Council. The Premier praised SGCC's social reporting behavior and said that "enterprises must be responsible to society, and should be supervised by the public voluntarily." After his words, especially in recent years, the number of social responsibility reports issued by Chinese enterprises has risen considerably. People are quite pleased to learn about the enterprises' social, environmental, and sustainability actions. However, this satisfaction was soon diluted by a succession of serious industrial scandals in China, as mentioned in Chapter 1. The disappointment was followed by the question about the real motives of businesses in reporting their social performances. Before investigating managers' incentives to report in China, it is important to create a broader picture and to understand the theoretical basis of social reporting.

During the development of CSR and SAR, the intention of management to voluntarily provide social information to outsiders has been widely discussed in Western academia (Foster and Jonker, 2005; Haniffa and Cooke, 2005). As shown in Figure 2.1, several theories are often used to explain this behavior. Among them, legitimacy theory (LT) and stakeholder theory (ST) have been adopted by many scholars (Mousa, 2010; Deegan, 2002; Gray et al., 1995). They are referred to as the "systems-oriented theories" (Gray et al., 1996). Within a system-based perspective, SAR is considered as a strategy to influence enterprises' relationships with other parties in society (Gray et al., 1996). Under LT, the main purpose for an organization to disclose social information is to prove that it is obeying the rules and to show that it operates within the law (Patten, 1992). On the other hand, ST focuses more on the rights of stakeholders. It emphasizes that social reporting is driven by the demand from various interested parties, such as

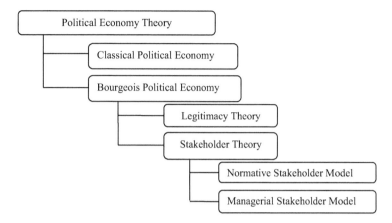

*Figure 2.1* The development of SAR theories

owners, investors, suppliers, employees, and so on (O'Dwyer, 2006). According to Gray et al. (1996), both theories have their roots in the political economy theory (PET) as shown in Figure 2.1.

### Political economy theory (PET)

PET posits that society, politics, and economies are indivisible. Any economic issue cannot be analyzed independently without political, social, and institutional considerations. Gray et al. (1996) have labeled two broad streams of PET: the classical political economy (CPE) and the bourgeois political economy (BPE). According to Karl Marx's work in 1867, CPE focuses on the structural conflicts within society (Marx, 1990). In this school of thought, SAR is considered a means of maintaining the interests of the bourgeoisie and undermining the power of the proletariat. In contrast, BPE does not deal with structural conflicts and class struggles. Instead, it emphasizes the interaction among groups in an "essentially pluralistic world" (Gray et al., 1995).

In the 1990s, the bourgeois form of PET was popular in the SAR literature (Guthrie and Parker, 1990; Williams, 1999). Guthrie and Parker (1990) conducted a comparative study of CSR disclosure practices in Australia, the United Kingdom, and the United States using the content analysis method. They argued that an organization uses social reporting as a means to mediate and accommodate the interests of recipients in a pluralistic society. Moreover, in line with PET, their result shows that corporations only disclose information that is not against their self-interest. Another empirical study conducted by Williams (1999) tests the BPE theory. He suggests voluntary social reporting provided by organizations is mainly for the purpose of protecting the reporting entities' self-interest under political and social pressures.

## Legitimacy theory (LT)

Both LT and ST are derived from BPE theory (Deegan et al., 2000). LT indicates that organizations disclose CSR information in order to tell the public they have taken some socially desirable actions and from this, intend to get approval from society in running their business.

A number of studies have provided evidence in support of LT. Due to space limitation, only three representative researches are discussed in this section. Deegan et al. (2002) examined CSR reporting of BHP Limited, a large Australian mining company. The objective was to investigate whether social disclosures were in response to major social concerns. Their results indicated that corporations disclosed a large quantity of CSR information for issues that received the highest media attention. Deegan et al.'s (2000) study also supports LT. They found that companies disclose more legitimate information in response to major incidents.

A further research conducted by Lewis and Unerman (1999) uses LT to explain the managerial incentive for SAR. They suggests that companies should integrate legitimization strategies into the social reporting process when facing different legitimacy threats, for instance, industrial accidents or financial scandals. While LT is widely applied by many SAR scholars, Deegan (2002) pointed out a gap within the LT literature, suggesting that as society is composed of different groups with unequal powers, LT fails to explain how enterprises respond to different groups within society, for example, whether any particular groups are more important to reporting entities and receive more legitimating disclosures than others. This gap was filled by stakeholder theory as discussed in following section (Belal, 2008).

## Stakeholder theory (ST)

The most widely used definition of a stakeholder is "any group or individual who can affect or is affected by the achievement of the organization's objectives" (Belal, 2008; Freeman, 1984). From this perspective, long-term survival of corporations requires the support and approval of their business activities by the stakeholders. Social reporting is treated as a kind of communication among the company and its stakeholders (Gray et al., 1995). As shown in Figure 2.1, there are two branches of stakeholder theory (ST): a normative branch and a managerial branch.

The normative branch claims the interests of all stakeholders should be treated fairly regardless of their "power" and have the same right to know the impact of the organization's activities on them (Deegan and Unerman, 2006). However, empirical studies have found little support for this branch. In contrast, several studies have provided evidence upholding the managerial model of ST (Belal, 2002; Deegan and Blomquist, 2001, 2006; Owen et al., 2000). This perspective suggests that enterprises would change their reporting behavior with the change of stakeholder power (Deegan and Blomquist, 2006). In other words, enterprises are more willing to make social disclosure to meet the demands of stakeholders who own more critical resources.

Based on the above discussion, many similarities can be found between LT and ST, as both of them emphasize "mediation, modification and transformation" but from different points of view (Belal, 2008, p. 13). As both of them are derived from PET, they should not be treated as two separate theories but two perspectives within a "political economy" framework.

## Development of social accounting and reporting

Similar to the process of theory development, the practice of SAR has also passed through a historical evolution. SAR is also known as social audit (Bauer and Fenn, 1973), social accounting (Epstein et al., 1976; Gray, 2000), corporate social (accounting) reporting (Dierkes and Preston, 1977; Dierkes, 1979; Preston, 1981; Gray et al., 1987; Gray, 2000; Gond and Herrbach, 2006), and corporate social (responsibility) disclosure (Guthrie and Mathews, 1985; Cowen et al., 1987; Belal, 2001). To help understand the nature of SAR, its origins must be considered.

In the early 1970s, there was no universally accepted definition of the field of social responsibility analysis. It was in 1973 that SAR was introduced to the world under the name of "social audit." It was defined as "a commitment to systematic assessment of and reporting on some meaningful, definable domain of a company's activities that have social impact" (Bauer and Fenn, 1973, p. 38). Given the importance of internal managerial and external accountability of a company in the mid-1970s, it was renamed "social accounting" and is defined as "the identification, measurement, monitoring and reporting of the social and economic effects of an institution on society" (Epstein et al., 1976, p. 24). Subsequently, a revised term, "corporate social accounting reporting" appeared in Dierkes and Preston's (1977) paper which was generated by "new demands" at that time. "The moment has come to provide an accounting base for the dialogue among the parties involved in the corporation, permitting measurement of social impacts and better setting of objectives. Such indicators permit the annual report to address itself to the social situation of the firm" (Beaudeux and Favard, 1975, p. 76). However, the debate developed when corporate social accounting and reporting was separated into two related concepts in the 1980s, with the one laying emphasis on the "process" called corporate social reporting (Gray et al., 1987) and the other placing stress on the "form" named as corporate social disclosure (Guthrie and Mathews, 1985). Corporate social disclosure can be defined as "the financial and non-financial information provided in annual reports or separate social reports relating to an organization's communication with its environment" (Guthrie and Mathews, 1985, p. 259), while corporate social reporting is clearly defined as "the process of communicating the social and environmental effects of organizations' economic actions to particular interest groups within society and to society at large" (Gray et al., 1987, p. 9).

Subsequently, with stakeholder engagement being taken more seriously in contemporary corporate social reporting, Gray (2000, p. 250) refined the earlier definition as "the preparation and publication of an account about an organization's social, environmental, employee, community, customer and other stakeholder interactions and activities and, where possible, the consequences of those interactions and activities." Recently, Belal (2008) conducted research in Bangladesh and summarized the aforementioned definitions particularly for developing countries. According to his interpretation, CSR reporting is "the external reporting of social, ethical and environmental aspects of a business organization." Although many scholars prefer to use sustainability reporting in their studies nowadays (which has been defined by Hubbard (2009) as "reporting by an organization on issues in relation to its social, environmental and sustainability performance"), the term "CSR reporting" adopted by Belal (2008) for developing countries is integrated with "social accounting" (Gray, 2000) in our research as SAR.

## The SAR model

Jones (2010) developed a theoretical framework to explain environmental reporting (one dimension of SAR). The model consists of five major layers: (1) environmental dangers, (2) corporate responsibility, (3) relationship between industry and environment, (4) a need to measure environmental impact, and (5) a need to report this impact. Additionally, there are eight underlying assumptions to explain and summarize the causal nexus. The model starts with the environmental threats that may lead to serious pollution. Given that the environmental change was brought by the great advances in human civilization (industrial development), industrial players have the duty to take socially responsible and legitimate actions. To accompany these actions, a measurement system is needed to assess the environmental impact caused by the companies' operations. However, current accounting is inadequate to serve this purpose. Therefore, a new holistic accounting was proposed for measuring the company's environmental impacts. Finally, it is argued that firms need to report environmental accounting information to stakeholders (Jones, 2010).

This model (Jones, 2010) is built based on the social environment of Western developed countries. Generally, it may also be relevant to the developing world. However, some developing countries within unique categories, especially China, which is within a socialist market economy with Chinese characteristics, may require a more complex model or framework of CSR reporting. In addition, regional differences also lead to differences in cultures, social structures, and political and economic systems. This aligns with the conclusion made by Hackston and Milne (1996, p. 78), which still holds nowadays, namely, "to date, however, there still exists no universally accepted theoretical framework of corporate social accounting."

## International SAR initiatives

Transparency of business operations is one of the most important responsibilities of any organization (Choi and Sami, 2012). In order to undertake this responsibility, companies would voluntarily disclose CSR information in their reports. To standardize the reporting process, two major global standards, the UN Global Compact and the GRI's reporting framework, are being developed and introduced. They list the indicators and initiatives that companies should apply to standardize non-financial reporting and to disclose their social impacts to interested stakeholders (Rasche and Kell, 2010).

The UN Global Compact[2] was announced by UN Secretary-General Kofi Annan in the late 1990s. This is the largest global CSR initiative, and it integrates a variety of stakeholders in a voluntary network that includes the United Nations as an authoritative facilitator. All stakeholder groups share the common goal of achieving sustainable development by embracing 10 fundamental principles concerning human rights, labor standards, protection of the environment, and anti-corruption.

To realize the principles, the UN Global Compact as a voluntary initiative does not rely on formal regulatory instruments. The companies that have joined the Compact are obliged to publish annual reports disclosing how the principles are being put into practice. These reports are made public through the UN Global Compact website. The names of the companies that have not published their respective annual reports are also announced there. As to the question of how exactly companies should report their sustainable development and the observance of the 10 principles, the UN Global Compact recommends some reporting guidelines offered by the Global Reporting Initiative (GRI).

> GRI is *"a multi-stakeholder process and independent institution whose mission is to develop and disseminate globally applicable Sustainability Reporting Guidelines for voluntary use which started in 1997. It became independent in 2002, and is an official collaborating center of the United Nations Environment Program and works in cooperation with UN Global Compact."*
>
> (www.globalreporting.org/AboutGRI/)

GRI has developed a series of guidelines for social reporting. The G3 guidelines (see Appendix 3), the third generation of GRI's framework, were released in 2006. The guidelines provide guidance on "sustainability reporting" so as to develop concrete indicators that make it possible to measure and assess a company's social performance. The indicators are arranged according to the following six groups:

1. The **economic performance indicators** measure the company's impacts on "the economic conditions of its stakeholders and on economic systems at local, national, and global levels" (GRI, 2006, p. 25).
2. The **environmental performance indicators** measure the organization's impacts on the natural systems, namely, "the performance related to inputs (e.g. material, energy, water), outputs (e.g. emissions, effluents, waste), biodiversity, environmental compliance, and other relevant information such as environmental expenditure and the impacts of products and services" (GRI, 2006, p. 27).

3   The **labor practices and decent work performance** indicators are based on internationally recognized standards related to labor and management relations, occupant health and safety, training and education, and so on.
4   The **human rights performance** indicators measure the extent to which human rights are considered in organizations' practices.
5   The **society performance** indicators refer to community, corruption, anti-competitive behavior, and so on.
6   The **product responsibility performance** indicators measure the organization's performance in areas such as consumer health and safety, marketing communications, and consumer privacy.

According to the guidelines, the report should include the following three main sections:

•   Strategy and profile of the company: "Disclosures that set the overall context for understanding organizational performance such as its strategy, profile and governance" (GRI, 2006, p. 20).
•   Management approach: "Disclosures that cover how an organization addresses a given set of topics in order to provide context for understanding performance in a specific area" (GRI, 2006, p. 24).
•   Performance indicators: "Indicators that elicit comparable information on the economic, environmental and social performance of the organization" (GRI, 2006, p. 24).

GRI represents probably the most generally accepted current social reporting guidelines at the international level. There are currently several domestic initiatives developed by the government and social organizations in China, and many of them make reference to GRI in order to comply with international reporting practices. Hence, GRI's reporting framework is used as an indicator system to evaluate the CSR reporting practices of Chinese enterprises in our study.

## Research approach

The Responsible Competitiveness Framework (AA and WTO, 2009) initiated by the Institute of Social and Ethical Accountability points out that the development of a social reporting system is consolidated by the contribution of policy makers, business people, and advocates of a civilized society. The framework implies that social reporting of enterprises in China may not be exclusively led by the government; it may be partly driven by the needs of organizational expansion as well as pressure from various stakeholder groups. Therefore, a comprehensive content analysis of annual reports and social reports published by enterprises in China is one source of information in this study that will explore possible answers to the research questions raised in Chapter 1.

In addition, to provide a more complete set of findings, the triangulation approach used is broadly defined as "the combination of methodologies in the study of the same phenomenon" (Denzin, 1978, p. 291). Webb et al. (1966, p. 3) recommended that "once a proposition has been confirmed by two or more independent measurement processes, the uncertainty of its interpretation is greatly reduced. The most persuasive evidence comes through a triangulation of measurement processes." Therefore, in addition to content analysis, regression and interview analyses are conducted in this research to offer the prospect of enhanced confidence.

Chapters 4 and 10 include the detailed research methods and the process applied in the study, respectively. By combining both qualitative and quantitative measures, the findings of this research can reliably address the main objective of this study, which is to explore and explain the CSR reporting motivations and practices of enterprises operating in China. Accordingly, content analysis on annual and social reports as presented in Chapter 4 to 9 are the major focus in this study, while the regression and interview analyses conducted for triangulating and reconciling the content analysis results are contained in Chapter 10.

## Notes

1  Yuan Jiafang published *Corporate Social Responsibility*, the first Chinese CSR monograph.
2  Official website of United Nations Global Compact, available at www.unglobalcom pact.org/AboutTheGC/index.html.

# 3 Institutional environment and legal system of CSR

## Introduction

Researches show that compliance with regulations or industry environmental codes are a major driving force for companies to report CSR information (Dias-Sardinha and Reijnders, 2001; Porter and van der Linde, 1995). Many countries have clear legal provisions for SAR. For example, the United Kingdom (UK) has issued several laws and regulations, such as the Regulation on Health and Safety at Work, the Employment Protection Act, the Law on Safety and Quality of Water Resource, and so on to mandate the scope of information being disclosed by public companies to stakeholders. France launched the *Nouvelles Regulations Economiques* to listed companies to disclose information on labor, health and safety, environment, rights of local society, human rights, and community issues within their annual reports since 2002. For China, the second-largest economy in the world, SAR has started to become an important agenda being highlighted in the various national congresses or conferences. This chapter introduces the structure of the institutional environment of SAR and the legal norms related to CSR in China. The purpose is to provide a legal and institutional basis of the research work that will be reported in the following chapters.

## Administrative and governance system in China

Since 2000, China has gradually been undertaking an institutional reform of CSR (see Appendix 2). The purpose is to establish a more civilized business environment. The reform originated from the call of governmental bureaus and authorities and was supported by many industrial associations as well as some research institutions, as shown in Figure 3.1.

CSR is the firm's obligation to society. It is also considered as a kind of right that can be claimed by stakeholders. The legal system plays an important role in regulating CSR practices that restrict the enterprise's behaviors and protect stakeholders' rights. In other words, the legal system is also an essential tool for regulating a firm's CSR practices and for ensuring the firm meets the legal requirements during the SAR process.

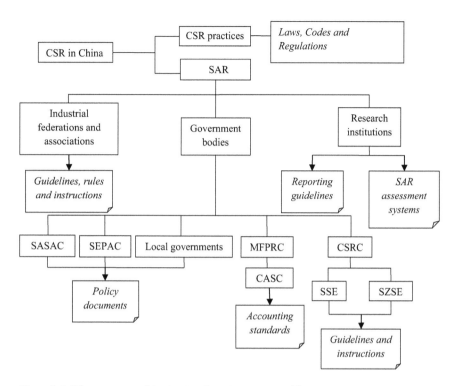

*Figure 3.1* The structure of institutional environment in China

SASAC: The State-owned Assets Supervision and Administration Commission of the State Council

SEPAS: The State Environmental Protection Administration of China

MFPRC: Ministry of Finance of the People's Republic of China

CSRC: China Securities Regulatory Commission

First, laws regulate bearing bodies, major elements and the basic form of CSR which establishes the foundation of legal security. It is stated in Article 5 of the Company Law of the People's Republic of China that "in conducting its business, a company must abide by laws and administrative rules and regulations, observe social morals and business ethics, conduct businesses in good faith, subject itself to the supervision of the government and the public and fulfill social responsibilities."

Second, the laws have emphasized the implementation of core CSR elements, peremptory norms, and penalties on violations. Examples of peremptory norms are labor standards, safety standards, environmental standards, hygienic standards, product quality standards, and so on.

Third, the government provides preferential treatment to socially responsible enterprises in the areas of tax, credit and loan, joint venture, franchise, and so on.

In this way, the government encourages Chinese enterprises to fulfill their social responsibilities.

Last but not least, many procedures in the legal sphere have provided conditions for enterprises to fulfill their social responsibility. For example, protecting employees' rights, collective negotiation, and democratic participation have become important issues for communications between the management and grassroots levels.

## Legal norms with CSR ingredients

### Constitution and law

The Chinese government attaches great importance and devotes effort to establishing and improving its social security system. In the constitution of the People's Republic of China, human rights and social development have been stipulated in the way that "the state shall establish and improve a social security system corresponding to the level of economic development" (www.gov.cn).

Additionally, corresponding laws have evolved for various CSR dimensions. For example, the "Labour Law" and "Labour Contract Law" are for the labor aspect; the "Environmental Protection Law," "Law on the Prevention and Control of Atmospheric Pollution," "Law on Environmental Noise Pollution Prevention and Control" are for environmental protection; the "Production Safety Law" and "Mine Safety Law" are for occupational safety and health; while the "Law on the Protection of Consumer Rights and Interests" is for consumers' rights.

### Administrative or local laws and regulations

Administrative regulations adopted by the State Council of the PRC (SCPRC) have the strongest legal authority in China. The SCPRC mainly makes national and general regulations or rules with CSR contents which are known as "ordinances" (in Chinese, *tiaoli*). These ordinances also play a significant role in temporary law. According to the departmental policies and Guidelines of the SCPRC (www.chinalaw.gov.cn), it is stated that legal documents mandated by each department of the SCPRC (e.g. Department of Commerce, Ministry of Labor and Social Security, National Development and Reform Commission, State-owned Assets Supervision and Administration Commission, Safety Inspection Bureau, Environmental Protection Administration, State Administration for Industry and Commerce and so on) should abide with CSR, in terms of international trade, labor employment, production safety, environmental protection, anti-bribery and so on (see Table 3.1).

Local laws, regulations as well as regional governmental rules are passed by provinces, autonomous regions, local people's congresses or standing committees. These authorities stipulate the implementation details of CSR according to the actual local or regional conditions which may also include some special or complementary provisions.

*Table 3.1* Summary of laws with CSR ingredients

| Law | CSR dimensions | Effective date | Last revision |
|---|---|---|---|
| Constitution | Comprehensive aspects (mainly focus on human right protection) | 4/12/1982 | 2004 |
| Company Law | Comprehensive aspects | 1/7/1994 | 2013 |
| Law on the Protection of Disabled Persons | Human right protection, Social security | 13/5/1991 | 2008 |
| Law on the Protection of Minors | Human right protection | 4/9/1999 | 2007 |
| Law on the Protection of Rights and Interests of Women | Human right | 1/10/1992 | 2005 |
| Labor Law | Protection of labor force, employment promotion | 1/1/1995 | N/A |
| Employment Promotion Law | Employment promotion, protection of labor force | 1/1/2008 | N/A |
| Social Insurance Law | Protection of labor force, social security | 1/7/2011 | N/A |
| Law on employment Contract | Employee protection | 1/1/2008 | N/A |
| Trade Union Law | Employee protection | 3/4/1992 | 2001 |
| Law on the Prevention and Control of Occupational Diseases | Employee protection | 1/5/2002 | 2011 |
| Production Safety Law | Production safety, employee protection | 1/11/2002 | N/A |
| Law on Safety in Mines | Production safety, employee protection | 1/5/1993 | 2013 |
| Law on Promoting Clean Production | Production safety, environmental protection | 1/1/2003 | 1/7/2012 |
| Standardization Law | Production safety, environmental protection, employee protection, consumer protection | 1/4/1989 | In progress |
| Environmental Protection Law | Environmental protection | 26/12/1989 | 2015 |
| Marine Environmental Protection Law | Environmental protection | 1/3/1983 | 2013 |
| Law on Appraising of Environmental Impacts | Environmental protection | 1/9/2003 | N/A |
| Law on the Prevention and Control of Environmental Pollution by Solid Wastes | Environmental protection | 4/1/1996 | 2005 |

(*Continued*)

*Table 3.1* (Continued)

| Law | CSR dimensions | Effective date | Last revision |
|---|---|---|---|
| Law on the Prevention and Control of Water Pollution | Environmental protection | 1/11/1984 | 2008 |
| Law on the Prevention and Control of Atmospheric Pollution | Environmental protection | 1/6/1988 | 2000 |
| Energy Conservation Law | Environmental and resource protection | 1/1/1988 | 2008 |
| Mineral Resources Law | Environmental and resource protection | 1/10/1986 | 1996 |
| Law on the Protection of the Rights and Interests of Consumers | Protection of consumers' rights and interests | 1/1/1994 | In progress |
| Real Rights Law | Protection of consumers' rights and interests | 1/10/2007 | N/A |
| Law on Product Quality | Protection of consumers' rights and interests | 1/9/1993 | 2000 |
| Anti-unfair Competition Law | Consumer protection, anti-commerce bribery | 1/12/1993 | In progress |
| Law on Anti-money Laundering | Anti-corruption and anti-commerce bribery | 1/1/2007 | N/A |
| Law on Donations for Public Welfare | Charity donation, social security | 1/9/1999 | N/A |
| Enterprise Income Tax Law | Charity donation, protection of labor force | 1/1/2008 | N/A |

## Legislation on stakeholders

China's current legislation on CSR is relatively scattered (see Table 3.1). This section sorts out the laws and regulations based on stakeholder theory as discussed in Chapter 2.

### Creditors

The responsibility for creditors has always been a core component of CSR, this is mainly governed by the "Contract law"[1] and "Guarantee law."[2] The core is that the enterprise must effectively fulfill the law of the contract to secure transactions. Contract Law despite the intention to involve CSR, it states some terms indirectly provide the basis and support for enterprises to implement public welfare and donations.

In addition, it also protects the interests of creditors by establishing a system separated from the corporate entity. Generally speaking, the company should be solely responsible for its debts with all its assets. This means that shareholders only need to bear limited liabilities equal to their capital contributions. The limited liability system is too much an emphasis on the protection of shareholders' interests which appears unfair to creditors. In view of this, the Company Law[3] introduces a system of disregard of the corporate entity. Additionally, the Enterprise Bankruptcy Law[4] provides a way to protect creditors in some special cases of corporate insolvency.

*Employee/labor*

China's laws on labor protection include "Labor Contract Law,"[5] "Social Insurance Law,"[6] "Company Law," " Reference 4), 709–738Dynamic income, progressive taxes, and the timing of charitable contributions, The Journal of Political EcoIndividual Proprietorship Enterprises Law,"[7] "Labor Law,"[8] "Law on Chinese-Foreign Contractual Joint Ventures,"[9] "Law on Foreign Capital Enterprises,"[10] and so on. Among them, the Labor Law specifically deals with the promotion of employment, labor contracts and collective contracts, working hours and breaks, wages, labor safety and health, female workers and special protection on underage workers, professional training, social insurance and welfare, labor disputes, and so on. The Labor Contract Law stipulates the rights and obligations of the parties regarding the conclusion, performance, alteration, and termination of the labor contract as well as collective contracts, labor dispatch, part-time employment, and so on. In another words, the law indirectly regulates the social responsibility that should be taken by a company for their employees. The Social Insurance Law states that the employer shall purchase the basic retirement security, basic medical insurance, employment injury insurance, unemployment insurance, and maternity insurance for their staff. It also mentions that employees have the right to enjoy social insurance benefits.

The Company Law, the Law on Chinese-Foreign Contractual Joint Ventures, and the Law on Foreign Capital Enterprises mainly stipulate the protection of workers through several articles. Two important aspects are covered, namely, the employer's responsibility on labor protection and a clear staff participation system. The staff participation system is one of the most important institutional measures to promote the implementation of labor protection. It mainly includes the employee-director system and staff supervisory system. Through the placement of employees in supervisory boards and boards of directors, it tries to include more stakeholders without controlling interests in the decision-making process of the organization to safeguard the legal rights and interests of the employees.

It is not difficult to find here that the existing laws lack special provisions for employees from small and medium-sized enterprises. First, the contents of labor protection apply to all enterprises; however, the applicable subjects are not discriminated on the companies' scale. Second, the staff participation system plays a very limited role. The system provides a platform or channels for employees to express their legal rights and interests in the process of business management. It is conducive to balancing the interests of shareholders and employees so as to avoid a hostile takeover by shareholders. Generally, the staff participation system is effective when staff representatives can participate in the decision-making process. However, in small and medium-sized enterprises, especially individual industrial and commercial households, their governance structures are not perfect. Many of them do not have boards of directors or supervisory boards. Therefore, it is difficult to provide effective legal protection for the employees of these entities.

### Consumer

The "consumer" here refers to individuals or organizations who purchase goods or services in the business environment rather than those who buy goods or services just for the needs of their life. The law on consumer protection mainly includes the "Law on the Protection of Consumers' Rights and Interests,"[11] the "Product Quality Law,"[12] and the "Food Safety Law,"[13] which are applicable to all types of enterprises. Similar to labor protection, no particular article is designated for the unique social responsibilities of small and medium-sized enterprises.

The Law on the Protection of Consumers' Right and Interests (Article 7–25) stipulates consumers' security rights, right to know, right to choose, fair trade rights, right to obtain compensation, and so on. Additionally, it has a universal provision on business operators' law-abiding obligations that includes the obligation on providing safe products, remedying defective products, providing factual product information, quality assurance, and other related aspects. Articles 3–5, 12–14, and 26–41 of the Product Quality Law are related to an implied guarantee on product quality by the producer, packaging of special products, and prohibition of adulteration. The law also specifies the responsibilities and obligations of sellers on goods inspection and product quality maintenance. The Food Safety Law (Article 27–41) sets provisions related to consumer protection, such as food production and management requirements, prohibited foods, audit permission on safety conditions, record system of food purchase inspection, and so on.

### Society and community

CSR on society and community is mainly reflected by legislation on environmental protection. Years of extensive economic development have led to serious environmental problems in China. The deterioration of the ecological environment and unreasonable use of resources have brought significant negative impacts on people's lives. The reason for this phenomena is China's reform and opening up placing too much emphasis on economic growth while ignoring the importance of sustainable development. In addition, both consumption and production patterns only focus on the present and do not consider the future. Moving toward the goal of sustainable development requires us to address environmental issues, change the traditional patterns of consumption and production, fully utilize resources, and promote resources recycling.

Protection of the environment has become a basic national policy. Building up resource-saving and environment-friendly enterprises is also an inevitable requirement if China is going to move toward sustainable development and to building a harmonious society. Some laws stipulate the responsibilities of enterprises to protect the environment, including the "Environmental Protection Law,"[14] the "Law on the Prevention and Control of Environmental Noise Pollution,"[15] the "Law on the Prevention and Control of Environmental Pollution Caused by Solid Waste,"[16] and the "Law on Conserving Energy."[17]

Articles 6, 40, and 42–43 of the Environmental Protection Law specify the principal responsibilities of enterprises. Articles 7, 13–19, and 22–47 of the Law on the Prevention and Control of Environmental Noise Pollution set forth provisions on the prevention and control of industrial noise, construction noise, traffic noise, and social-life noise pollution. Articles 9 and 16–66 of the Law on the Prevention and Control of Environmental Pollution Caused by Solid Waste stipulate specific provisions on the prevention and control of pollution on industrial solid waste, domestic waste, hazardous waste, and so on. Articles 9 and 24–28 of the Law on Conserving Energy regulate the energy units' obligations, such as establishing an energy-saving responsibility system, providing regular energy-saving education, and providing post-energy training.

### Market players

CSR on supplier, competitor, and other business stakeholders is mainly related to a firm's market responsibilities, which are integrated in the "Company Law," the "Antitrust Law,"[18] the "Contract Law," the "Law against Unfair Competition,"[19] the "Partnership Law,"[20] and the "Law on Individual Sole-Proprietorship Enterprise."[21] Articles 7, 10–11, 21, 25, 37–42, and 88–92 of the Partnership Law sets forth provisions for competitors, creditors, and other market players. This law also states the requirements for partnership enterprises on maintaining social and economic order and promoting the development of the socialist market economy. However, its contents are scattered and general. Articles 9, 173–176, and 185–186 of the Company Law stipulate contents on changes of corporate responsibility, responsibility towards stakeholders in merger, division, and dissolution and liquidation scenarios. Articles 13–17 and 20–21 of the Antitrust Law clearly define the behaviors on restricting market competition, such as on reaching a monopoly agreement and the abuse of a dominant market position. Articles 5–15 of the Law against Unfair Competition provides detailed provisions on an operator's disruption of the market order and infringement on other enterprises' legal rights and interests. Articles 3–5, 60–76, and 107–122 of the Contract Law present provisions on the establishment, effectiveness, fulfillment, change, transfer, termination, and breach of contracts. The law also contains articles on sales contracts, commissioned contracts, lease contracts, and other provisions.

## Other aspects

In addition to the provisions on the protection of employees, consumers, society as a whole, and market players, the existing laws also cover the tax and donation systems. Tax incentives are the most representative arrangement in the donation preferential system, which also positively affects the implementation of CSR. The donation system is closely linked with CSR. Theoretically, people believe that CSR is an important basis for regulating corporate charitable donations, which is a kind of persuasive responsibility (Diamond, 2006). Therefore, to direct the enterprises' fulfillment of this part of social responsibility, incentive mechanisms and institutional arrangements are vital (Bakija and Heim, 2011). It is also recognized that donation is an effective way for improving a business's image, which is conducive to the company's long-term development (Randolph, 1995).

## Conclusion

Although so far China does not have formal laws or ordinances to regulate SAR, initiatives, instructions, policy documents (see Appendix 2) as well as various laws mentioned in this chapter do form a legal basis for the purpose. The Chinese government and regulatory bodies are proactively improving the system, and they continually play an external supervisory role to guide enterprises in the implementation of CSR and its disclosure. Nevertheless, the effectiveness of this regulatory approach is not clear and leaves much to be investigated in the chapters that follow.

## Notes

1  Contract law is available at www.gov.cn/banshi/2005-07/11/content_13695.htm.
2  Guarantee law is available at www.gov.cn/banshi/2005-09/01/content_68752.htm.
3  Company Law is available at www.gov.cn/flfg/2006-10/29/content_85478.htm.
4  Enterprise Bankruptcy Law is available at www.gov.cn/jrzg/2006-08/28/content_371 055.htm.
5  Labor Contract Law is available at www.gov.cn/banshi/2005-05/25/content_905.htm.
6  Social Insurance Law is available is available at www.law-lib.com/law/law_view.asp?id=327704.
7  Individual Proprietorship Enterprises Law is available at www.npc.gov.cn/wxzl/wxzl/2000-12/05/content_4750.htm.
8  Labor Law is available at www.gov.cn/banshi/2005-08/31/content_74649.htm.
9  Law on Chinese-Foreign Contractual Joint Ventures is available at www.gov.cn/banshi/2005-08/31/content_69772.htm.
10  Law on Foreign Capital Enterprises is available at www.gov.cn/banshi/2005-08/31/content_69774.htm.
11  Law on the Protection of Consumer's Rights and Interests is available at www.gov.cn/banshi/2005-08/31/content_68770.htm.
12  Product Quality Law is available at www.sda.gov.cn/WS01/CL0784/91772.html.
13  Food Safety Law is available at www.gov.cn/banshi/2005-08/31/content_68767.htm.
14  Environmental Protection Law is available at zfs.mep.gov.cn/fl/201404/t20140425_271040.htm.

15 Law on the Prevention and Control of Environmental Noise Pollution is available at www.gov.cn/ziliao/flfg/2005-08/05/content_20921.htm.
16 Law on the Prevention and Control of Environmental Pollution Caused by Solid Waste is available at www.zhb.gov.cn/gzfw_13107/zcfg/fl/201605/t20160522_343380.shtml.
17 Law on Conserving Energy is available at www.gov.cn/banshi/2005-08/31/content_68768.htm.
18 Antitrust Law is available at www.law-lib.com/law/law_view.asp?id=212679.
19 Law against Unfair Competition is available at www.gov.cn/banshi/2005-08/31/content_68766.htm.
20 Partnership Law is available at www.gov.cn/banshi/2005-08/31/content_68746.htm.
21 Law on Individual Sole-Proprietorship Enterprise is available at www.npc.gov.cn/wxzl/gongbao/2000-12/05/content_5004750.htm

# 4 CSR reporting of state-owned enterprises

## An overall perspective

## Introduction

With the promotion of a market economy in China and the implementation of a strategy for sustainability development, the CSR awareness of the Chinese people has become stronger. The public, therefore, not only cares about the tax revenue generated by the government but also wants to know the contributions made by enterprises in the areas of environmental protection, social welfare, safety, and charity (Chen and Ma, 2005). At the same time, stakeholders call for comprehensive and transparent reporting of social information. Among Chinese firms, state-owned enterprises (SOEs) are the backbone of the country's economic development. Therefore, the status quo of the SOEs' SAR attracts much louder attention from the public. This chapter introduces the SOEs' stages of development in SAR, investigates the quantity and quality of their social reporting contents, and explores the underlying causes.

## Stages of development

The SOEs have gone through more than 60 years of development. Meanwhile, their CSR reporting has demonstrated significant changes. In summary, they have experienced three main stages: the "social function stage," the "value retaining and increment stage," and the "all-round development stage" (Qiao and Liu, 2010; Wang, D., 2010; Fan, 2012).

### Social function stage (Qiao and Liu, 2010)

From 1949 to 1978, before the Third Plenary Session of the 11th Central Committee, the CSR activities of SOEs mainly focused on social functions. During this time, state ownership and collective ownership were the only two ownership types of Chinese enterprises. Due to the behindhand economy and inadequate functions of government bodies, SOEs were required to support various social functions (e.g., employment, staff housing, children's education, health and pension, and so on) besides realizing economic growth and meeting social needs. At that time, a large-sized SOE was actually a small society. Within this small society, the SOE itself took most of the social responsibilities of the state. In the field of SAR, SOEs treated social functions and responsibilities as their own business. They did not have any concept of CSR. They only disclosed some information in internal communiqué, which we now call "CSR information," such as the menus of workers' canteens, various entertainment programs, activities for retired employees, and so on. From a different point of view, it is satirical, as SOEs of that time really took the ownership of CSR and SAR. People lived in the total care of their SOE within the small society or community, and that was the kind of society expected during that era (Xu et al., 2011).

### Value retaining and increment stage (Qiao and Liu, 2010; Wang, D., 2010)

From 1978 to 1998, there was a round of SOE reform. Following the Third Plenary Session of the 11th Central Committee, the planned economy in China started to transform toward a market economy. Various enterprises with different ownership types appeared in the market. SOEs faced severe competition from private and foreign sectors, and their financial performance decreased markedly. They were overburdened by the immense cost of fulfilling social functions. Many of them relieved the pain by cutbacks and layoffs. Many SOEs incurred years of deficit and survived by relying on the state's financial support. They became a heavy burden to the country. The state successively adopted the contract responsibility system in management and other political approaches, freeing SOEs from social functions so as to revitalize them. At this stage, the Chinese economy experienced rapid development, and the priority of SOEs was placed on retaining and increasing their own value. For this reason, SOEs turned into profit-seeking entities after some of their burden of social functions was removed. Under loosened control by the government, they started to focus on creating wealth instead of fulfilling social responsibilities.

### All-round development stage (Qiao and Liu, 2010; Fan, 2012)

Since the beginning of the 21st century, SOEs experienced further growth in business scale and financial performance. However, it is arguable that CSR was neglected by SOEs due to their pursuit of economic benefits. Problems like production safety, product quality, and environmental pollution appeared with increasing regularity. This not only had damaged SOEs' image but also had negatively impact on their daily operations. The financial success in business actually created a huge contrast with the lack of social responsibility.

Since the late 1990s, a tidal wave for the CSR movement rose globally, which ignited China's attention to it (Branco and Rodrigues, 2008; Zhang et al., 2009). The Chinese public placed new expectations on the social responsibilities taken by SOEs. This stimulated a new CSR era for SOEs (Tao, 2013). In 2002, GRI was translated into Chinese and introduced to public companies. In 2000, PetroChina Company Limited published the first report of health, safety, and environment, which gained significant attention from the public. Later on, more and more SOEs produced similar reports to communicate their social responsibility information and activities with stakeholders. In 2006, State Grid Corporation of China issued the first social report, which symbolized the beginning of their CSR reporting stage. In the same year, the State-owned Assets Supervision and Administration Commission (SASAC) held several meetings to discuss the CSR issues of SOEs and drew up a list of measures. Afterward, they released the "Guidelines to the State-owned Enterprises Directly under the Central Government on Fulfilling Corporate Social Responsibilities" (Guideline, 2006). These guidelines required SOEs to "integrate CSR with their own reform and development, and regarded the implementation of CSR as an important content of setting up a modern enterprise system and enhancing their competitiveness" (Guidelines, 2006). The guidelines also clarified SOEs' responsibilities in various aspects, such as product and service quality, energy conservation, environmental protection, production safety, labor right, charity issues, and so on. In response to the government's call, a large number of SAR initiatives, policy documents, instructions, and guidelines have appeared since 2006. As such, we have taken 2006 as the starting year for the study of contemporary SAR in China.

### Pressures from government and regulatory bodies

As shown in Appendix 2, in 2006 the China Accounting Standards Committee (CASC) announced a set of revised accounting standards for enterprises (standards no. 5, 9, 16, and 27) requiring companies to "disclose relevant information for recognition and measurement of biological assets related to the agricultural production, employee compensation, government subsidies and exploitation of petroleum and natural gas." This is the first set of mandatory standards about SAR, although it only covers very limited CSR dimensions. During the same year, the Shenzhen Stock Exchange (SZSE) released "Social Responsibility Instructions for Listed Companies" in order to encourage public companies to prepare CSR reports voluntarily on a regular basis. In 2008, the peak of the SAR reform, three mandatory documents about environmental disclosure were issued. They are "Environmental Information Disclosure Act" by the State Environmental Protection Administration (SEPA), "Guidelines on Environmental Information Disclosure by Companies Listed on the Shanghai Stock Exchange" by the Shanghai Stock Exchange (SSE), and "Notification on Issuance of the Guideline on Fulfilling Social Responsibility by Central Enterprises" by the SASAC. In response to the government's call, 11 national industrial federations and associations issued guidelines on "Social Responsibility for Industrial Corporations and Federations" to encourage all industrial companies (iron, steel, oil, chemicals, power, textiles, building materials, non-ferrous metals, electric power, and mining industries) to build a system with CSR reporting and performance indicators. Among these associations, the China National Textile and Apparel Council (CNTAC) plays a leading role, as textile accounts for a significant percentage of exports and improving SAR is an essential means for building a good business image for this industry. In 2008, CNTAC introduced "China Sustainability Reporting Guidelines for

Apparel and Textile Enterprises" and "China Sustainability Reporting Verification Rules and Instructions." Both initiatives aim to promote SAR and provide principles and instructions for textile and apparel enterprises to use in preparing CSR reports. Similarly, the China Banking Industry Association (CBIA) released "Guidelines on Corporate Social Responsibility for Banking Financial Institutions in China" in 2009 to advise all banks to produce CSR reports and submit them to CBIA annually. During the same year, in order to standardize the layout and performance indicators in reports produced by different industrial players, SASAC published "China Corporate Social Responsibility Reporting Guidelines" on an experimental basis. These guidelines serve as a local version of GRI to guide enterprises in conducting SAR on a voluntary basis. After two years of experimentation, SASAC improved these guidelines and issued a second version, which is considered as the first formal set of official SAR guidelines in China.

It is clear that the central government had spent a lot of effort on building a system of SAR and had vigorously encouraged Chinese enterprises to disclose CSR information to the public in recent years. In response to the government's call, the stock exchanges and several industrial regulatory bodies also initiated SAR instructions and guidelines to require or encourage CSR reporting. In recent years (2008–2012), enforcement of CSR has become stricter. This may be a result of the various industrial scandals that took place and a means to restore public confidence in Chinese enterprises. As reported in KPMG's 2011 survey, "At different press events, various high-level officials from SASAC stress that all SOEs must issue a 2011 CSR report in 2012" (KPMG, 2011, p. 24). This can be considered as an important underlying driver, which caused a dynamic increase in the number of social reports published during 2009–2010 (Figure 4.1). Under

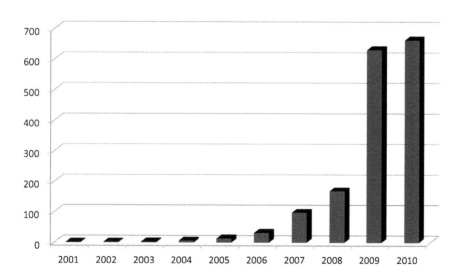

*Figure 4.1* Number of CSR Reports issued by listed enterprises in China
Source: KPMG (2011)

this circumstance, the quality and transparency of the CSR reports issued have attracted great attention by the public, such as the mass media, the NGOs, and various research institutions. Thereby the public's concern and interest have created a quasi-supervisory role in the SAR practices of Chinese enterprises.

## Content analysis based on GRI

According to Neumann (2003, p. 219), "content analysis is a technique for gathering and analyzing the content of texts. The content refers to words, meanings, pictures, symbols, ideas, themes, or messages that can be communicated" Holsti (1969, p. 14), provides a broader definition of content analysis as "any technique for making inferences by objectively and systematically identifying specified characteristics of messages." He states that "only the manifest attributes of texts may be coded. . . [from which] inferences about latent meanings of messages are permitted" (Holsti, 1969, p. 598). This technique has been widely used in the social reporting academia during the past decades (Gray et al., 1995; Adams et al., 1995; Adams and Harte, 1999; Perrini, 2006; Mirfazli, 2008).

In this research, both quantitative and qualitative approaches were applied. On the one hand, words, sentences, figures, and numbers in the reports related to the disclosure of CSR information were coded and recorded in a spreadsheet for statistical purposes. On the other hand, those words and sentences were further analyzed and reviewed to identify their underlying meanings. In this manner, managers' perceptions, intentions, or motivations behind the disclosure of CSR information can be explored.

### Sampling method

A combined stratified and cluster sampling selection method was adopted. A total of 535 annual reports and 247 social reports of 182 companies in China were selected for the period 2006–2010. These companies are from 14 industries categorized by the China Securities Regulatory Commission (CSRC) in 2001 (Si Tou and Noronha, 2015) and three different groups in terms of ownership types, namely, SOEs, private companies, and MNCs (foreign-invested companies). Annual reports and social reports were gathered from the SSE (www.sse.com.cn), the SZSE (www.szse.com.cn), and the companies' websites. In total, the whole research process involved at least 11,356 working hours for reading more than 82,254 pages of reports in order to conduct an in-depth analysis of social reporting practice of the observed enterprises. This chapter presents the investigation on SOEs, and the content analysis results of private and foreign-invested companies are presented in Chapters 7 and 9.

Two hundred ten annual reports and 117 CSR/sustainability reports published by 62 SOEs during 2006–2010 were selected for content analysis (see Table 4.1). The base document is a list of Chinese listed enterprises from 2006 to 2010 generated from CSMAR.[1] The list was sorted by year, industry, and capital size. An enterprise is classified as a SOE if its largest shareholder is an agent/affiliate of

*Table 4.1* Distribution of SOEs' annual reports and social reports selected

| Industry category | Industry name | Number of SOEs selected (Note 1) | Number of annual reports (2006–2010) | Number of standalone CSR reports and sustainability reports (Note 2) | | | | | |
|---|---|---|---|---|---|---|---|---|---|
| | | | | 2006 | 2007 | 2008 | 2009 | 2010 | Total |
| A | Agriculture, forestry, livestock farming and fishery | 4 | 15 | 0 | 0 | 0 | 0 | 0 | 0 |
| B | Mining | 5 | 15 | 1 | 2 | 4 | 3 | 3 | 13 |
| C-1 | Manufacturing (light) | 3 | 15 | 1 | 1 | 2 | 2 | 2 | 8 |
| C-2 | Manufacturing (heavy) | 3 | 15 | 0 | 0 | 3 | 2 | 3 | 8 |
| D | Electric power, gas, water production and supply | 3 | 15 | 1 | 1 | 2 | 3 | 3 | 10 |
| E | Construction | 6 | 15 | 0 | 0 | 2 | 3 | 3 | 8 |
| F | Transport and storage | 5 | 15 | 0 | 0 | 2 | 3 | 3 | 8 |
| G | Information Technology | 4 | 15 | 1 | 1 | 2 | 3 | 3 | 10 |
| H | Wholesale and retail trade | 6 | 15 | 1 | 1 | 2 | 3 | 3 | 10 |
| I | Finance and insurance | 4 | 15 | 1 | 2 | 4 | 4 | 4 | 15 |
| J | Real estate | 6 | 15 | 0 | 1 | 2 | 3 | 3 | 9 |
| K | Social service | 4 | 15 | 0 | 0 | 0 | 2 | 2 | 4 |
| L | Communication and Cultural Industry | 5 | 15 | 0 | 0 | 2 | 2 | 3 | 7 |
| M | Comprehensive | 4 | 15 | 0 | 0 | 2 | 2 | 3 | 7 |
| | Total | 62 | 210 | 6 | 9 | 29 | 35 | 38 | 117 |
| | Percentage of Total | 100% | 100% | 5% | 8% | 25% | 30% | 32% | 100% |

Note 1: The top three SOEs ranked by capital size of each industry were selected for each fiscal year. As each year's ranking may be different due to the changes of capital size, a SOE selected in the former year may be off the list in the later year and be replaced by a new one. Therefore, the total number of SOEs selected varied among industries.

Note 2: Some SOEs issued both CSR reports and sustainability reports

the state, local SASAC, or another SOE. To ensure the representativeness of the samples, for each fiscal year, the top three SOEs in terms of capital size were selected by industries. For private enterprises, similar sampling procedures were applied, except the base document was obtained from the website of All-China Federation of Industry and Commerce,[2] which is composed of the top 500 private enterprises from 2006 to 2010.

## Codification

A coding sheet was prepared based on the GRI-G3 checklist (www.globalreport ing.org), which includes a content index for social reporting. GRI is a widely accepted and acknowledged benchmark in the CSR reporting field because it can ensure comparability of the research results in relation to other studies in developing or socialist countries. Six trained coders analyzed and coded the data. For consistency purposes, a coding instruction consisting of rules for setting codes and examples was developed (Weber, 1990; Babbie, 2010). The coders were not informed of the content and design of the research. They were required to code the relevant information from annual reports and social reports in the coding sheet, including the number of CSR key words, the coverage of CSR dimensions, SOEs' attitudes to social reporting, and the bad news being disclosed. The coding rules in the study are summarized as follows:

- *CSR key words*. A list of key words in Chinese was prepared according to the content of the GRI-G3 guidelines. The coders counted the number of individual key words related to each CSR dimension (see the next bulleted item) in the Chinese annual reports and social reports. Two or more Chinese characters often represent one English noun. For example, "social responsibility" is formed by four Chinese characters – "社會責任 (she hui ze ren)," which is treated as one CSR key word in this study.
- *CSR dimensions*. Four dimensions of profile disclosures, six dimensions of performance indicators, and social reporting aspects of each dimension are listed in the coding sheet according to GRI-G3 (see Table 4.2). "1" is coded in the field of a CSR aspect if relevant information is disclosed in the selected report and "0" is coded for non-disclosure. Intensive training was provided to the coders to ensure their understanding of GRI.
- *CSR disclosure quality*. Quality is evaluated and ranked into five quintiles. "1" is coded if information presented is very general, without explanation or description; "2" is coded if information presented is general, with little description or explanation; "3" is coded if information presented is rough and

*Table 4.2* Summary of CSR dimensions

| Standard disclosure | Dimensions | Number of aspects* |
|---|---|---|
| Profile Disclosure | Strategy and Analysis (SA) | 20 |
| | Organizational Profile (OP) | 26 |
| | Report Parameters (RP) | 24 |
| | Governance, Commitments and Engagement (GCE) | 44 |
| | Economic (EC) | 3 |
| Performance Indicator | Environment (EN) | 9 |
| | Labor practices and decent work (LA) | 5 |
| | Human rights (HR) | 7 |
| | Society (SO) | 5 |
| | Product responsibility (PR) | 5 |

\* Profile disclosure is required in the general guideline of GRI-G3, which mainly consists of the four dimensions listed above. Aspects in each dimension of profile disclosure are counted and summarized by the authors in this study.

brief, with some description or explanation of issues; "4" is coded if information presented is specific, with detailed description or explanation of issues; "5" is coded if information presented is very specific, with detailed description or explanation and supporting monetary and statistical numbers or graphs.

## Reliability of data set

Although a fairly standardized procedure is used in the content analysis of this study, validation of the consistency of coding results produced by different coders is necessary and important (Babbie, 2010). Before starting the analysis, two tests were arranged. The coders were asked to code a sample report in each test and their judgments were checked and compared. The inter-coder agreement coefficient (IAC = agreements/[agreements + disagreements]) was 0.725 in the first-round test, which is slightly below the 0.8 rule of thumb for being good as suggested by Krippendorff (1980). Thus, any variances were resolved through discussions among the coders and the authors. In the second-round test, the coding consistency was improved, and the IAC increased to 0.874. After completion of the analysis, the same test was conducted and the result showed an IAC of 0.896, which means that 89.6 percent of the coding items were agreed upon by the coders.

Regarding external reliability, the most important aspect is to make sure that people agree that the reports are disclosing the same CSR phenomena and have a common understanding of them (Krippendorff, 1980; Babbie, 2010). That means CSR information or data disclosed in annual and social reports are about something real and factual. To measure the reliability of source information and data, 10 percent of the annual reports and social reports analyzed were randomly selected. Three evaluating procedures were performed on a sample of the data. First, the existence of third-party assurance was checked. As all the observations are listed or international companies, their annual reports were audited by independent CPA firms. Thus, the CSR information disclosed in an annual report is considered as more reliable than that in a social report, which is without third-party assurance. Second, information from the social reports was cross-checked with the annual reports and vice versa. Finally, if bad news or significant issues were disclosed, relevant information was further checked through the mass media, such as newspapers and the internet. The result of this evaluation procedure showed that 96.2 percent of 1,283 data items could be cross-checked in annual reports and social reports; 97.1 percent of 89 pieces of bad news and significant events was corroborated by relevant news reported by mass media. Therefore, both internal and external reliability for the data set can be assured.

## Content analysis results

### The overall reporting trend

Concerning the levels of CSR disclosure in the SOEs' annual reports (see Figure 4.2 and *Appendix 4*), six out of 10 categories (namely, organizational profile [OP], economic [EC], environment [EN], labor practices and decent work [LA],

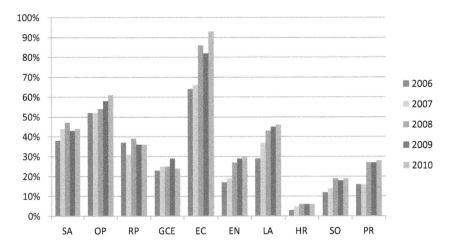

*Figure 4.2* Average coverage of CSR dimensions in 210 annual reports of the largest SOEs in China

Note: This column chart is composed based on the statistics in Appendix 4

society [SO], product responsibility [PR]) showed a general increasing trend in terms of the coverage of these CSR dimensions required by GRI. This is in line with our discussion in Chapter 3 about the fact that the government and its regulatory bodies have, since 2006, continuously required listed companies, especially SOEs, to disclose their CSR practices (see Appendix 2). As a result, the extent and variety of disclosed CSR information has increased. Additionally, in order to ensure the consistency of this finding, the number of CSR key words in the annual reports was counted by the year, and the result showed a similar increasing trend (see Figure 4.3). It indicated a rise in CSR disclosure quantity, which further demonstrates the SOEs' taking note of government initiatives and shows recognition of the government as their key stakeholder. That is, they have become increasingly aware of the government's policy documents and initiatives as well as its authority in the promotion of social reporting.

However, in contrast with the statistics of CSR reports shown in Figure 4.1, no sharp increase of CSR coverage was identified in the 2009 and 2010 annual reports. One possibility is that the SOEs focused highly on financial issues in their annual reports, as 2009–2010 was a critical period of economic recovery after the 2008 global financial crisis. Thus, they may not be so highly sensitive during that period to the enforcement of CSR initiatives by the central government, given the extent of the economic crisis. This is reflected in Figure 4.4, where the diversified CSR disclosure in annual reports was not accompanied by an increase in the reporting quantity of CSR dimensions. For further analysis, the statistics of social reports (see Figure 4.5) were checked. The overall trend, though not very obvious (most of the significant changes of reporting coverage in 2009 or 2010

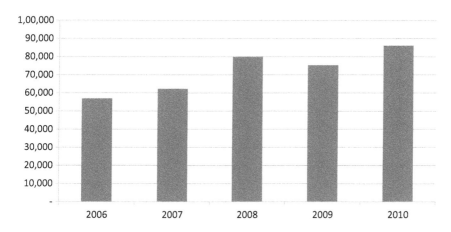

*Figure 4.3* Number of CSR key words disclosed in 210 annual reports of the largest SOEs in China

Note: This column chart is composed based on the statistics in Appendix 5

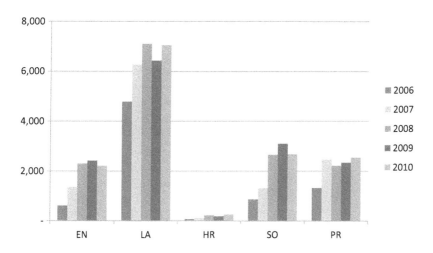

*Figure 4.4* Number of CSR key words disclosed in 210 annual reports of the largest SOEs in China by indicators

Note: This column chart is composed based on the statistics in Appendix 5

were distorted by 2008's sharp increase), showed category increments in 2009's RP, 2010's GCE, and 2010's EN, which were mainly driven by two major initiatives. In December 2009, CASS issued "China's Corporate Social Responsibility Reporting Guidelines," version 1.0. The main purpose was to educate Chinese enterprises on how to report and what should be reported. In the content of

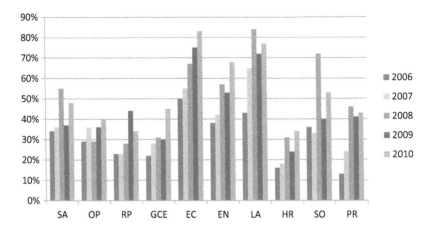

*Figure 4.5* Average coverage of CSR dimensions in 117 social reports of the largest SOEs
in China

Note: This column chart is composed based on the statistics in Appendix 5

the guideline, management approach, report scope, report boundary, governance, and commitments are emphasized; most of them can be reconciled with the relevant aspects in the RP and GCE dimensions of GRI.

In early 2010, the Chinese government announced the detailed targets of its 12th Five-Year Plan that mainly aimed at reducing greenhouse gas emissions by 40–45 percent. During the same period, in March 2010, SASAC issued "Interim Measures for Governing SOE Energy Saving and Emission Reduction." This event led to strong concern for environmental disclosure in the 2010 social reports, explaining the emphasis on EN mentioned above.

### Analysis of reporting quality

According to the content analysis results, the quality of CSR reporting of SOEs in both annual reports and social reports showed an increasing trend from 2006 to 2010 (see Figure 4.6). Although the SOEs' recognition of the importance of social reporting has improved and increased from 1.15 points in 2006 to 2.45 points in 2010, the average quality score up to 2010 has not yet reached 3 points. This implies that information presented is rough and brief, with some description or explanation of issues, which shows that CSR reporting of SOEs still has considerable room for further development. This finding is in line with the result of Kuo et al.'s (2011) research and is also similar to the findings in the case of Bangladesh (Belal, 2008), Indonesia (Mirfazli, 2008), India (Raman, 2006) and other developing countries. However, unlike these prior studies, this research is more focused on exploring the incentives and development trend or path of CSR reporting in China. Therefore, it is necessary to further break down the analysis

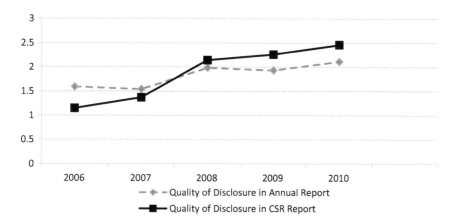

*Figure 4*.6  Overall quality of CSR disclosure in the largest SOEs in China from 210 annual
reports and 117 social reports

Note: This column chart is composed based on the statistics in Appendix 5

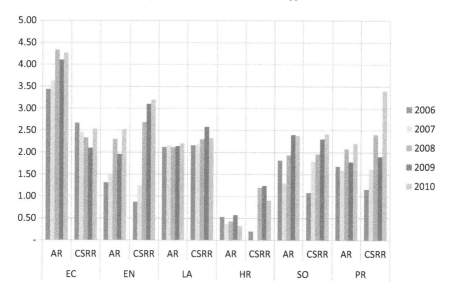

*Figure 4*.7  Average quality of CSR disclosure in the largest SOEs in China from 210
annual reports and 117 social reports

AR denotes annual report; SR denotes social reports

Note: This column chart is composed based on the statistics in Appendix 5

into CSR dimensions (see Figure 4.7). EC in annual reports (as financial issues
are the major topic in annual reports) is ignored; only EN and PR in social reports
exceeded the three-point level. Initially, it could be posited that SOEs undertake
social reporting activities with a very positive attitude. However, after exploring

the quality issue further, it was observed that a majority of the SOEs did not provide much detail in social reporting, as most of the information disclosed was rough and brief. In other words, their attitude on this was relatively superficial.

In addition, the causes of significant improvement in the disclosure quality of 2008's reports also warrant further exploration (see EN, HR, SO and PR in Figure 4.7). It would appear that the sharp increase in the quality score is mainly due to a vigorous drive staged by the central government and its authorities. However, there were also social pressures on this disclosure and through this a more thorough picture may be obtained. The milk powder scandal (see Chapter 1) was a critical driver that stimulated the government to release a considerable number of CSR and social reporting initiatives at the end of 2008 (*Appendix 2*). In response to the policy documents, Chinese enterprises produced more social reports and disclosed a wider range of CSR information, but the quality of disclosed information still left much to be desired.

In 2010, greater importance was found to be attached to the environmental and product responsibility issues in annual and social reports (see EN and PR in Figure 4.7). Despite the announcement of 12th Five-Year Plan targets in early 2010, another factor drove this behavior of the SOEs. In 2010, industrial scandals and serious pollution incidents shocked the entire Chinese society. The first was pork with an illegal additive, as mentioned in Chapter 1. The second was industrial wastewater leakage of Zijin Mining Group. The wastewater led to serious pollution in the main river in Fujian Province. This accident had caused about 378 kilograms of dead fish.[3] A further example relates to China National Petroleum Corporation. Two oil pipelines burst and leaded oil damaged the popular beaches and fisheries in Shandong Province, with smoke shrouding much of downtown Dalian.[4] Interestingly, many other SOEs, which were not involved in these scandals, also voluntarily disclosed more detailed information related to environmental and product responsibility issues in 2010. A possible explanation here is that they intended to distinguish themselves from those "bad images." It is also observed that for those SOEs with industrial accidents and scandals, the quality of disclosed information has subsequently been improved, probably in order to restore their reputation and image. However, "how to protect the environment" still occupied the main content of their social reports after the incidents that had brought such huge social costs. Still, not much disclosure of the aftermath of the incident was made. Even though scandals began to increase and were widely reported by the mass media in recent years, not much bad news was disclosed in the annual and social reports issued by the SOEs (see Appendix 6). All these findings could suggest that social reporting is effectively a window-dressing tool through which many SOEs are highly motivated to "whitewash" their image and with which those SOEs with bad news can try to improve their tarnished images.

## Conclusion

In summary, the content analysis results discussed in this chapter show the SOEs' rapid improvement on disclosure quantity. However, their progress in enriching the quality of their reports remained slow. This is mainly due to the fact that the SOEs are eager to improve their social reporting performance in response to the government's call. Unfortunately, the actual education on the act of CSR reporting was behind schedule during the same time (Wu, 2013). In 2007, the SASAC released "Guidance and Advice on the Fulfillment of Social Responsibilities." The guideline requires all SOEs to proactively exercise social responsibility and participate in activities that will set a good example for others. However, a complete domestic CSR reporting guideline was issued only very late in 2010 (see Appendix 2). SOEs were therefore challenged to produce a high-quality report without systematic training and deep understanding of the CSR reporting elements. Although the CSR reporting performance of SOEs still has left much to be desired and has a long way to go, the efforts of SOEs in this area can be clearly observed as analyzed in the previous sections, and they also keep enhancing their reporting quality and transparency by making reference to other CSR guidelines and initiatives. In addition, their practice did stimulate other public companies' awareness of CSR reporting (see Chapters 7 and 9).

As mentioned earlier, several important CSR policies announced in 2008 had driven the significant improvements in the SOEs' CSR reporting performance. Hence, thereafter, the total number of CSR reports issued by listed companies increased sharply in 2009 and 2010 (see Figure 4.1). Considering the close relationship between the central government and SOEs, it is believed that the government's policies have always been efficiently and properly interpreted and reflected in the SOEs' reports. In the following chapter, we move to more specific areas (such as industrial patterns and the accuracy of disclosure) for further analysis on the SOEs' SAR practices.

## Notes

1 CSMAR is "a leading global provider of China financial market data, China industries and economic data, whether real-time, delayed or historical (over 55 years for the latter two), to international financial and educational institutions." (www.gtafib.com/data-product/database.aspx)
2 Official website of All-China Federation of Industry and Commerce, available at www.acfic.org.cn/publicfiles/business/htmlfiles/qggsl/index.html.
3 News from the *Wall Street Journal* dated July 20, 2010, available at www.wsj.com/articles/SB10001424052748703724104575378813113956620.
4 News from BBC news dated July 21, 2010, available at www.bbc.com/news/world-asia-pacific-10708375.

# 5 CSR reporting of state-owned enterprises

## Some specifics and reporting trends

### Introduction

Based on the research approach outlined in Chapter 4, this chapter aims to detect the forces driving the SOEs' social reporting development based on industrial analysis and discussion of several other CSR issues identified during the content analysis process. Thus, in connection with the findings of Chapter 4, a unique route to reveal the SOEs' SAR behavior is being structured.

### CSR reporting in high-profile and low-profile industries

In the CSR literature, enterprises are commonly separated into high- or low-profile industries (Patten, 1992; Hackston and Milne, 1996). "High profile industries are those with consumer visibility, a high level of political risk, or concentrated intense competition" (Roberts, 1992, p. 598.), and their operating activities are expected to cause much impact on the economy, environment, and society (Newson and Deegan, 2002). Several researchers conclude that high-profile enterprises reported more CSR information than low-profile enterprises (Roberts, 1992; Choi, 1999; Ho and Taylor, 2007). In this research, according to the situation in China and the global market, the following five industries are categorized as high-profile industries: mining, heavy manufacturing, utility, finance and insurance, and real estate (Gunawan, 2010; CIEL, 2008). The others are classified as low-profile industries. To compare the CSR reporting behavior of SOEs in high-profile and low-profile industries in China, a Chi-square test was conducted that yielded two $\chi^2$-values of 61.495 (p=0.002) for annual reports and 85.523 (p=0.000) for social reports, respectively. Data were collected based on the content analysis results from 2006 to 2010. They indicated that a significant difference existed between the CSR reporting practices of high-profile and low-profile SOEs. The analysis was further broken down into CSR indicators and aspects. Table 5.1 shows, on average, a larger percentage of high-profile SOEs report social information in each dimension relative to that of low-profile SOEs. This demonstrates that high-profile enterprises tended to disclose more CSR information, and the difference was more obvious in social reports than annual reports. This finding is in line with the results of prior studies that show that industry nature is a factor affecting corporate

Table 5.1 Comparison of coverage in CSR dimensions between SOEs in high-profile and low-profile industries in China

| CSR performance indicator (number of aspects) | Annual report | | | Social reports | | |
|---|---|---|---|---|---|---|
| | High-profile SOEs Percentage of total n = 75 (number of SOEs) | Low-profile SOEs Percentage of total n = 135 (number of SOEs) | Chi-square Test $\chi^2$-value (p-value) | High-profile SOEs Percentage of total n = 50 (number of SOEs) | Low-profile SOEs Percentage of total n = 67 (number of SOEs) | Chi-square Test $\chi^2$-value (p-value) |
| EC (3) | 83% (62) | 76% (102) | 0.031 (0.9846) | 89% (45) | 52% (33) | 16.752*** (0.0002) |
| EN (9) | 82% (61) | 20% (28) | 20.123*** (0.0099) | 62% (31) | 48% (30) | 20.237*** (0.0095) |
| LA (5) | 61% (46) | 22% (30) | 10.809** (0.0288) | 76% (38) | 67% (42) | 17.951*** (0.0013) |
| HR (7) | 12% (9) | 1% (2) | 9.409 (0.1518) | 18% (9) | 34% (21) | 7.364 (0.2885) |
| SO (5) | 79% (59) | 19% (25) | 12.582** (0.0135) | 52% (26) | 12% (8) | 10.030** (0.0399) |
| PR (5) | 60% (45) | 20% (27) | 8.541* (0.0737) | 36% (18) | 9% (6) | 13.189** (0.0104) |

Note: Significant at the *0.1, **0.05, ***0.01 levels, respectively

social reporting (Hackston and Milne, 1996; Dierkes and Preston, 1977). Furthermore, a significant distinction was identified between these two groups of SOEs in the dimensions of EN ($\chi^2$-values =20.123, p=0.0099 and 20.237, p=0.0095), labor ($\chi^2$-values=10.809, p=0.0288 and 17.951, p=0.0013), society ($\chi^2$-values=12.582, p=0.0135 and 10.030, p=0.0399) and product responsibility ($\chi^2$-values=8.541, p=0.0737 and 13.189, p=0.0104).

The occurrence of this phenomenon (level of disclosure) can be shown to align with the pronouncements of trade organizations and industrial regulatory bodies during the observed period of 2006–2008, such as the China National Textile and Apparel Council (CNTAC) and the China Banking Industry Association (CBIA) (see Appendix 2). Especially in 2006, the CNTAC established the example of Chinese industries issuing social responsibility reports; in 2007, the China Banking Regulatory Commission (CBRC) issued "Opinions on Strengthening the Social Responsibilities of Financial Institutions in the Banking Sector"; in 2009, the China Federation of Industrial Economics (CFIE) issued social reports at the Great Hall of the People, which created a platform for the issuance of CSR reports by industrial companies and organizations. As shown in Figure 5.1, the SAR ranking is in the decreasing sequence in terms of CSR risks of the industries. The top five SAR performers are companies from B-mining, I-finance and insurance, D-energy and utility, and C-2 and C-1 manufacturing (heavy and light). All these industries are in the high-profile sectors and under strong control of the government.

The government and its agencies as well as industrial organizations generally pay significant attention to enterprises fulfilling their social responsibility. In recent years, they have released a series of policy documents, guidelines, and instructions to provide support and encouragement for Chinese enterprises to develop social reporting. This applies especially to SOEs. In addition to the policy documents listed in *Appendix 2*, in 2008, the State Asset Regulatory

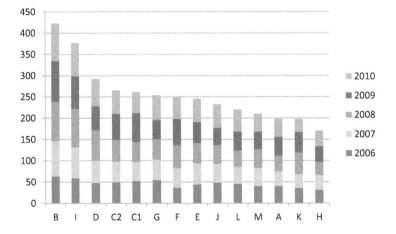

*Figure 5.1* Ranking of CSR reporting by industries

Note: This figure is generated based on the statistics in Appendix 7

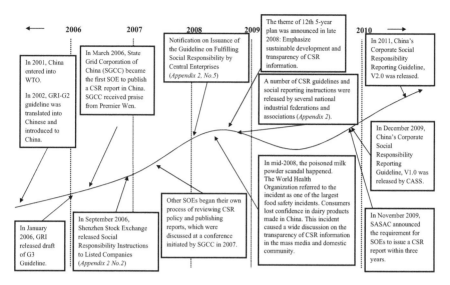

*Figure 5.2* Chronological sketch of social reporting development in China

Commission of the State Council issued the "Guidelines for Central Enterprises to Fulfill Social Responsibilities," in which the social responsibilities of central SOEs were clearly laid out (Li and Liu, 2010). This is also an important factor that drives the increase in the coverage of CSR dimensions in social reports (e.g., EN, LA, HR, SO, and PR) in 2008 (see Chapter 4). All these findings further confirm the proposition raised earlier that the promotion of social reporting is strongly driven by the Chinese government. SOEs can be seen to have continuously increased the extent and coverage of CSR disclosure in their annual reports and have issued more CSR reports to the public over the period 2006–2010.

A sketch in Figure 5.2 is used to illustrate a chronology of social reporting in China and acts as an important basis for creating an overview of its development. The bold curve in the center represents a trend of CSR disclosure quantity (*see* Figure 4.3) and quality (*see* Figure 4.6) of SOEs during 2006–2010. Figure 5.2 also points out the major events that caused attention to be given to CSR issues by the national government, international guidelines, and the coverage by the mass media and Chinese society. These point out the major events that had brought CSR increasingly onto the agenda of businesses generally and SOEs in particular.

## Other findings based on the qualitative analysis of SOEs' CSR Reports

### *Tax – a corporate responsibility priority*

China's constitution stated that urban land is owned by the state. A document released by the Ministry of Land and Resources in 1998 specified that during the process of land reform, each SOE is required to calculate the value of state-owned land they leased from the state and turn over to the state treasury the relevant rent income (Document, 1998). However, a grey area exists in this statement. That is, if there is no reform, the SOEs can continuously occupy the state-owned land without any charge by the central government. To avoid dissenting voices from other types of enterprises, the SOEs are required to pay a five percent business tax on any rental income (www.chinatax.gov.cn).

For example, a SOE from the chemical industry (the Group) obtained a piece of land (420 million square meters) from the state and lent it to one of its subsidiaries for operating use in 2004. In return, the subsidiary pays rent to the Group and the Group needs to pay business tax accounting for five percent on the rental income to the State Taxation Administration. To calculate the business tax, the determination of the per-square-meter rental rate is very important. However, related information is absent in this subsidiary's annual reports or social reports, which means the accuracy of the rental rate cannot be ascertained. In addition, as shown in the Group's annual reports, they recorded a certain amount of lease prepayment for land use rights paid to the government. However, the nature and uses of the land were not mentioned in the notes to their financial statements. To pursue this story further, the price of the land the subsidiary leased from the Group could only be found in the 2004 annual report. The rate was RMB12.38 per square meter. No further disclosure was identified in the 2005 annual report or later reports. The group made a revaluation adjustment of land use rights but no adjustment on the rental rate charged to the subsidiary. This led to a significant amount of understatement when calculating the five percent business tax. This is a typical case of a tax issue. Actually, during the content analysis process, we found that many other SOEs have similar practices. Most of them are from heavy industries, such as steel, mining, and power companies. Moreover, the rents for mineral resources, such as oil, coal, and natural gas have the same problem in rate determination.

Additionally, the SASAC issued the "Advice on Deepening the Reform of Internal Personnel, Labor and Distribution Systems" in 2002. The advice states that SOEs have the right to set salary levels for their staff based on profit levels and average wages in the local market (Advice, 2002). As mentioned earlier in this section, SOEs do not pay rent for state-owned land, which can help them save money and increase profit. Salaries of high-level managers are connected with the profits made by SOEs. Therefore, there is a potential conflict of interest, or an agency issue, because part of the rent savings from state-owned land is being turned into managers' bonuses in the end.

### Equity incentive scheme for high-level management

The SASAC has another document, the "Implementation of Stock Option Incentive for State-controlled Listed Companies (Trial)," which was announced in 2006. It is mentioned that SOEs can use stock options to motivate high-level managers. The maximum quantity is one percent of the total number of shares, which is close to 30–40 percent of their annual salary (Document, 2006). This document sets off a round of split-share structure reform among SOEs. Eighty-three percent of SOEs disclosed information about the equity incentive scheme in their annual reports in 2006. For example, in the annual report of an electrical appliance manufacturer, it is stated that their group provided 26.39 million shares of the company to management-level personnel. The selling price of shares equals to the audited net asset value at the end of the year. However, issuance of share options in large quantities may cause management faults, such as insider dealings and earnings management. The central government issued this policy document with the purpose of providing a kind of "staff benefit" to good performers. However, the government should realize that this equity incentive scheme might impair the interests of other medium and small investors and lead to unethical behaviors of high-level managers in SOEs. For example, to boost a company's stock price, managers may intentionally overstate the reported profit through manipulations in order to exercise their stock options.

Based on the remunerations disclosed in the SOEs' annual reports, the annual salary growth rate of senior executives was around 14 percent from 2006 to 2010. For instance, in 2009, the average annual salary of CEOs of selected SOEs was about USD 90,000.[1] Many of them also hold other positions and receive allowances from shareholders or affiliates. Thus, it is difficult to understand the reason why the central government still encourages SOEs to implement equity incentive schemes for high-level managers.

### Environmental provisions versus government subsidies

In the annual reports of high-pollution industries (e.g., oil, coal mine, power, steel), we can find provisions for environmental issues as potential liabilities. However, most of the SOEs have also frequently recorded an item called "government subsidy or grant" as an offset with the cost or expense of part of their reserve in capital. Taking a large state-owned oil company as an example, according to their disclosure in the annual reports, the company paid normal routine pollutant discharge fees and other environmental contingencies fees of around RMB 3 billion to the government every year from 2007 to 2010. Superficially, it seems the company compensates society for environmental damages that might be caused by its production. But in fact it also received financial subsidies from the government in the average amount of RMB 1 billion every year from 2008 to 2010 after the first grant of RMB 1.11 billion in 2007. In the 2008 annual report, the company explained that the government provided the financial subsidy to "secure the market supply" of crude oil and oil products. From this rough explanation, it is difficult to get the meaning of "securing the market supply," especially without any description of the relevant event, if any. The actual situation is that the company has sufficient financial capacity to handle its oil business. As shown in the 2008 income statement, the company's net profit accounted for around RMB 113.8 billion. Other energy and utility companies are in a similar situation, receiving government subsidies while retaining high profits.

## Conclusion

Based on the findings in Chapters 4 and 5, the state-owned economy is considered a key part of the economic system during the transitional period. Indeed, the leading role of the SOEs is written into many of the policy reports of the central government and the CPC national congress. This has also been proven by the content analysis results. Thus, SOEs are naturally treated as a kind of ruling foundation or tool of the government, on the one hand, to grow the economy and GDP, and on the other hand, to promote SAR and to build a strong CSR environment in China. However, due to the lack of training and professional human resources, the SAR quality of SOEs leaves much to be desired. In addition, the related government authorities should draw attention to the hidden issues mentioned in this chapter. Otherwise SAR is more like a window dressing instrument than a value-adding tool for improving market performance.

## Note

1 News from Xinhua Net dated March 12, 2010, available at www.yn.xinhuanet.com/employment/2010-03/12/content_19231766.htm.

# 6  The social roles of private enterprises

## Introduction

Private enterprises have become China's largest business group, accounting for more than 60 percent of Chinese companies. They absorb more than 80 percent of new employment every year, and their output accounts for over 50 percent of the GDP. In addition, private enterprises make significant contributions to the country by providing around 50 percent of the research and development (R&D) funding, 70 percent of the R&D personnel, over 60 percent of invention patents, more than 70 percent of new product development, and numerous well-known brands.[1] As an important component of China's economy, private enterprises bear many social responsibilities. They play a very important role in adjusting the industrial structure, promoting social harmony, and helping the country to achieve remarkable economic development during the last three decades (Li and Zhan, 2012). In order to introduce more details of the CSR background of private enterprises, this chapter intends to discuss the social role and capital nature of private enterprises and conducts a longitudinal review of the critical issues related to the CSR performance of private firms in China.

## Historical background of Chinese private enterprises

The birth of private enterprises in China is mainly due to the "reform and opening up" policy.[2] The development of the private sector can be seen as a process from small to large and weak to strong, and has gone through the following four stages.

The first stage is the start-up stage. The Third Plenary Session of the 11th Central Committee of the Communist Party of China led China's economic reform, and the private economy began to emerge at that time (Di, 2015). In 1979, when Deng Xiaoping[3] met with the vice chairman of the editorial board of the American *Encyclopedia Britannica*, Deng said: "Socialism can also engage in a market economy" (Di, 2015). Therefore it was necessary to break the dominance of state ownership and develop private enterprises. The first private enterprise, Guangcai Limited, was founded on April 13, 1984, by Jiang Wei in Dalian City, marking the beginning of the start-up phase of private enterprises in China (Xu and Zhou, 2011).

The second stage is the growth stage. The late 1980s to the early 1990s was a very difficult time period for the private sector, which experienced a significant decline during that time. Until 1992, Deng Xiaoping put forward the "three favorable" criteria in a speech during his southern China tour. They are, he said, "whether it ("it" here refers to a private company) (1) promotes the growth of the productive forces in a socialist society, (2) increases the overall strength of the socialist state, and (3) raises the people's living standards" (Di, 2015). These three criteria became an important measure of the merits and demerits of all social and economic work. They were also treated as a guideline for private enterprises' future development. China has thus increased the intensity of reform and opening up. Economic development had been moving quickly, and the private economy had a stable external growth environment during that decade (Sun, 2010).

The third stage is the mature stage, which was from the mid-1990s to the end of the century. In 1997, the 15th Party Congress proposed that the non-public economy, such as the individual and private enterprises, should be continuously encouraged and guided to create healthy development.[4] During this period, the private economy obtained more favorable policies, and the privatization of some state-owned enterprises strengthened the manpower of the private sector. However, the structural reform of the SOEs had also led to a large number of laid-off workers, which became a new challenge for private enterprises.

The fourth stage is the expansion stage, which was from the early 2000s until now. This era is marked by several critical political issues, such as the initial establishment of the socialist market economic system, China's accession to the WTO, and the 16th, 17th, and 18th National Congresses of the Communist Party of China (NCCPC). All the above mentioned NCCPCs had emphasized to "unswervingly encourage, support and guide the development of the non-public economy."[5] This policy brings broader space and greater opportunities for the future development of private enterprises.

## The capital nature of Chinese private enterprises

No specific definition has been given to private enterprise in Western academia. Only the basic meaning of "private" has been stated, which simply means private business (Zhu, 2002). In China, since the reform and opening up in 1978, the private economy was established and developed from the contract responsibility system in rural areas. to private businesses with a certain scale and then to private joint-stock companies. Therefore, private enterprise is a special concept under the specific socioeconomic conditions in China. This form of business can be treated as an institutional arrangement to replace the SOEs and adjust property rights in China.

In the Chinese economic academia, there are different schools of thought on the capital nature of private enterprises. Some believe that this form of business simply represents legal economic entities that can enjoy investment income and also need to bear the related risk (Ji, 2011). However, another school of thought divides private enterprises into state-owned private and purely private companies (Wang and Li, 2005). For the former one, although the owners operate their companies independently and finance the business by themselves, the property rights belong to the state, while the latter refers to business invested by individuals and with purely private ownership. Therefore, as in the Western world, the primary objective of Chinese private enterprises is also to pursue profit maximization. Their investment behavior is mainly driven by the market, and capital is always transferred to those products with stronger demand (Wang and Li, 2005). Compared to SOEs, the mechanism of private enterprises is more flexible in managing the labor force, investment, production, sales, and product distribution (Xu and Zhou, 2011). These flexibilities create strong competitive advantage. Moreover, most private entrepreneurs have a great entrepreneurial spirit that makes the entire economic sector full of vitality.

## The social role of Chinese private enterprises

Private enterprises are an important part of the economy and one of the mainstays of the socialist market economy. Private enterprises also play a social function in the process of building a harmonious socialist society, especially in the continuous improvement of the market economy and the common development of various economic components of China (Hu et al., 2013).

Private enterprises, on the one hand, actively play their economic functions, such as creating profits and economic value, mediating internal and external interests, maintaining staff team cohesion, and promoting economic development, employment, prosperity, and other related aspects. On the other hand, they also actively carry out important social functions, consciously assume social ethics and moral responsibility, and actively participate in social undertakings, exercise ethical functions, and strive to play a certain role in social harmony (Hu et al., 2013). The harmonious social role of private enterprises is related not only to the harmonious development of themselves but also to the harmonious progress of society as a whole (Jiang et al., 2006).

### The origin of social responsibility of private enterprises

The concept of social responsibility of private enterprises has extended from the general sense of CSR as discussed in Chapter 2, and thus it has some common features with what people usually think of social responsibility. However, it also has a certain uniqueness due to its internal structure, ownership form, social environment, development mode, and so on. The private economy and private enterprises are a unique form of business in China. No relevant information can be found in modern Western economic theories. "Private" refers to the common people. Private economy, as suggested by the name, represents the main body of the economy, that is, the people (Lu, 2002).

As with state-owned or state-controlled enterprises, private firms have independent legal person ownership according to civil law. Companies established in China that do not belong to the state-owned, state-controlled, collective, collective holding, or foreign invested enterprises are classified as private enterprises

(Lu, 2002). They may include joint-stock cooperative systems, non-state-owned joint ventures, collective joint ventures, state-owned and collective joint ventures, non-state-owned limited liability companies, joint stock limited companies, private enterprises, individual sole proprietorships, individual partnerships, and self-employed companies (Lu, 2002).

Since the 1990s, Chinese enterprises began to be exposed to CSR issues after entering into the supply chain of overseas markets. More than 8,000 private companies have accepted the required social responsibility audit as required by foreign multinationals. Firms with better social performance were able to receive more orders. Some companies were disqualified as authorized suppliers due to the lack of improvement in CSR (Yang, 2013).

Starting from the late 1990s, with the development of China's foreign trade and foreign exchange, the international CSR movement was introduced into China. At that time, many foreign multinational companies have developed hundreds of production codes, and Chinese exporters were required to be certified. This new requirement had a great impact on Chinese export-oriented enterprises, among which the majority were private companies. It has also caused widespread concerns and discussions in the mainland

After 2000, almost all European and American companies had to assess and review the social responsibilities of their global suppliers. At present, exports from China to Europe and the United States, including clothing, toys, footwear, furniture, sports equipment, and household hardware are constrained by the SA8000. In the forefront of exports, Chinese private enterprises have experienced considerable pressure. Therefore, the issue of CSR has become critical during the internationalization process of private companies.

### The status quo

The existence of private enterprises improved the overall competitiveness of China's economy. They have made tremendous contributions toward China's social and economic development. Since the reform and opening up, especially after the 15th National Congress of the Communist Party of China, the role of private enterprises in China's economic arena have become more and more important. According to statistics, the number of private enterprises has amounted to more than 80 million, with at least 200 million employees. Their contribution to the GDP growth accounts for more than 60 percent, which has largely determined the development of the national economy.[6]

However, private enterprises as a product of the economy's transition, treated economic function as the core of their businesses, which means the only goal is to pursue profit maximization and the companies' own interests. Because they sought only economic benefits, a sense of responsibility and moral standard tended to become scarce. Therefore, when implementing business strategies, private enterprises took all the means and methods to maximize corporate sales and profits, which often neglected social and moral aspects. Some private enterprises pursued economic benefits regardless of environmental destruction, plundering natural resources, damaging harmonious relationships, and even conducting business at the expense of others and the interests of society. They produce and sell fake and shoddy products and even disregard human life. The continuous occurrence of coal-mine accidents is an obvious example.

On the other hand, there are still many reputable and law-abiding socially responsible private enterprises and private entrepreneurs. They engage in ethical business activities, repay the community, and fulfill their social responsibilities. Numerous private enterprises actively participated in the Guangcai program initiated by Chinese private entrepreneurs. They make investments in social projects and public welfare donations, participate in employment and re-employment, provide village twinning help, and participate in new rural construction and other aspects of public welfare. According to statistics, as of 2011, the Guangcai program has collected RMB 22.9 billion in donations (around USD 3.5 billion), trained 1.03 million workers, made employment arrangements for 1.04 million people, and helped more than 2.5 million people to get out of poverty.[7] They have played an important role in narrowing the economic and social development gap between the eastern and the western regions in China and accelerating the regional economic development of poverty-stricken areas. Private enterprises have also participated in various social activities, such as organizing forums, seminars, and lectures to fulfill their social responsibility and promote the healthy development of private economy. For example, in 2007, "enhancing social responsibility and promoting social harmony" became the theme of the sixth Private Enterprise Forum for the first time. During the forum, the "Declaration on social responsibilities of private enterprises" was published as an initiative for the earnest fulfillment of social responsibilities by private companies.[8]

## Existing problems

A large group of private enterprises has completed the capital transition process since China's reform and opening up. They have the economic conditions and advantages for further development and expansion. Their growth is mainly based on low-cost competition. Many private enterprises exploit, deduct, and delay the payment of wages. They also wantonly extend the working hours of their employees and ignore violations in the production environment and security, which may lead to serious pollution and significant waste of resources. In addition, some ethical problems also exist in the private sector, such as lack of credit, fraud, tax evasion, violation of intellectual property rights, and production of fake products. Thus, ignoring corporate social responsibility has become a serious problem for Chinese private enterprises and the biggest obstacle to the sustainable development of this sector (Jiang et al., 2006).

### Lack of credit

In the current Chinese market economy, credit management in the private sector is experiencing a crisis (Li and Zhan, 2012). Some credit scandals, such as breach of contract, fraud, and other unethical phenomena, happen frequently and are difficult to stop. These unethical industrial and commercial activities will inevitably bring harm to society. In some severe cases, they cause deaths and seriously interfere with the normal market economic order.

The problem is mainly reflected in the following four aspects.

The first aspect is contract default and contract fraud. In accordance with the provisions of the Contract Law, the parties shall fulfill their obligations completely in accordance with the stipulations. However, there are still many enterprises that do not seriously take action according to their signed contracts or agreements. Some companies deliberately conceal the facts or provide false information when making a contract.

The second aspect is the manufacturing and selling of shoddy products, which have created unfair competition. It not only violates consumers' legal rights and interests but also disrupts the social and economic order. This behavior has become the object of a crackdown in China. However, it is still continuously occurring despite repeated prohibitions. The government has conducted investigations of nearly 300 famous enterprises in 2013. These enterprises had about 650 kinds of famous products being counterfeited (www.stats.gov.cn/). Fake dens spread all over 490 cities and regions. Some counterfeit goods are even sold at much higher prices than the original products. For example, in Wenzhou, counterfeit, inferior shoes could be found everywhere.[9] Other scandals, like fake alcohol in Shuozhou city of Shanxi province[10] and cakes with expired fillings produced by Guanshengyuan in Nanjing[11] has even shocked the whole food and beverage industry in China.

Infringement of registered trademark and patent rights is the third aspect. To promote technological progress and protect the legal rights and interests of business operators, China has enacted and promulgated the "Patent Law"[12] and "Trademark Law".[13] These two laws stipulate that no person shall use patented technology and registered trademarks without the permission of the patentee and the trademark owner. However, many companies ignore the law. They impersonate others' registered trademarks and use patented technology without authorization, causing huge losses to patentees and trademark owners.

The fourth aspect is the disclosure of false information, providing false proofs and shady transactions. These phenomena have frequently happened in the service industry and the commodity trading and investment areas, such as the widely reported stock market investment scandals like "Zheng Baiwen"[14] and "Yin Guangxia."[15] These dishonest behaviors lead to a weak sense of trust of Chinese customers or even international consumers.

### High energy consumption and serious pollution

In terms of energy consumption and material consumption, Chinese private enterprises are relatively high. According to statistics, China's energy consumption for each US dollar of output is 4.3 times more than that of the United States, 7.7 times of Germany and France, and 11.5 times of Japan (Zhu et al., 2013).

Additionally, recycling technology and awareness is far behind those of developed countries. At present, China's energy utilization rate is 33 percent, industrial water recycling rate is 55 percent, and total recovery rate of mineral resources is 30 percent, which are lower than the advanced levels in foreign countries by 10 percent, 25 percent, and 20 percent, respectively.[16] The excessive utilization of natural resources will eventually negatively affect the interests of future generations. The radical and extensive growth mode leaves much to be desired for the development of a harmonious society

Some private enterprises disregard the regulations on the discharge of waste materials. To reduce production costs and operating expenses, large quantities of industrial sewage, exhaust gas, and waste materials are poured into rivers, released to the atmosphere, and thrown into the soil, activities that have led to irreparable damage to the environment. Some serious impacts are impossible to be measured in monetary terms.

### Human rights and labor protection

Employees are the most valuable resources of a company. The key for achieving long-term business development is employees' enthusiasm and creativity (Ghosh, 2015). Enterprises and their labor providers have to form a harmonious relationship. Therefore, respect for human rights and protection of industrial health and safety are essential social responsibilities to be borne by business operators. At present, many private enterprises have not established a people-oriented corporate culture. They extend working hours, reduce labor insurance, and deduct wages to cut operating costs. In addition, business operators and managers ignore the poor working conditions and safety of their staff, blindly reduce labor prices, prolong labor time, reduce labor costs, and ignore the rights and interests of workers. These phenomena are mainly caused by the long period of oversupplied labor force in the country's history. Before 2005, labor-intensive enterprises had set a very low standard on the quality of the labor force, causing China's "strong capital" and "weak labor" economic development (Wang, 2015). Enterprises could recruit workers with low wages and poor working conditions. Workers found it difficult to put forward their own demands democratically, and they could not even consider asking for any labor protection.

### Tax evasion and lack of charitable activities

The economic and social functions of private enterprises are mainly for the community to increasingly create sufficient materials for securing (1) the operation of the national economy, (2) the normal functioning of the central and local governments at all levels, and (3) the supply of required materials for all types of enterprises and institutions (Wang and Li, 2005). In other words, their basic social responsibility is to protect social interests and support social development by providing substances in demand. On the other hand, as a major taxpayer group, they indirectly contribute to the capital accumulation of the state and rapid development of the national infrastructure through tax fulfillment. Therefore, paying tax is another type of basic social responsibility that is also a statutory requirement for private enterprises. In addition, enterprises should also support and make donations to social welfare or charitable undertakings as an extension of their social responsibilities.

The extant problem is that some private enterprises have been "distressed" by the taxes paid, leading to many tax evasion measures. For example, they reduce taxable income by inflating costs. They also take advantage of the tax incentives for high technology and small businesses by re-registering a new enterprise with the same business nature every two to three years. With the further development of the market economy, the financial and taxation system will become much stricter. In this context, even if the entities with tax evasion do not consider potential legal risks and credit risks, they will find it difficult to adjust their accounts to conceal earnings manipulation. Sometimes, the external financing process of a company can be seriously affected. For example, if a company intends to be listed in the stock exchange, their past three years of accounts need to be assured by external auditor. Tax evasion is a serious problem that may cause the external auditor to issue adverse opinions. This indicates that the firm's financial records do not conform to accounting standards or legal requirements. In addition, the financial records provided by the business may have been grossly misrepresented or may reveal accounting fraud.

In terms of the charitable aspect, many private enterprises are not accustomed to participating in social welfare activities, and they even consider this part of their work as their additional burden (Yang, 2013). In fact, participation in social activities is an important aspect of private enterprises' CSR. Water, electricity, roads, health care, and other public facilities enjoyed by enterprises are provided by society and are also inseparable from the local government and community's support. Therefore, enterprises have the obligation to provide social services, such as making investments or providing human resources to help the community to develop education, health, transportation, and other infrastructure so as to improve people's living environment.

### Poor production environment

Some private enterprises do not attach importance to labor safety and protection. Due to poor management, fire, explosion, physical trauma, and other accidents happen frequently, especially in the mining, construction, and other manufacturing sectors (Li, 2014). The production sites of these companies often fail to install proper labor protection facilities. Their employees are exposed to occupational hazards in the poor production environment during working hours. In addition, a considerable number of small to medium-sized enterprises have not established or improved safety management systems and procedures. Some companies have basic security systems and operational norms, but they only remain at a superficial level. For instance, security personnel are far from being desired;

safety procedures are not strictly followed and implemented. According to statistics, in the event of security incidents, production safety accidents caused by staff violations of operating procedures and labor discipline accounted for more than half of the total number of accidents (Yang, 2013).

### Weak social security

The private enterprises that purchase endowment insurance for their staff account for a very low portion among the whole population (Li, 2015). Normally, only management-level personnel are entitled to be insured. The front-line employees are given very limited social security. Additionally, medical insurance and unemployment insurance are seldom purchased by private companies for their staff. The social security problem makes many people unwilling to find jobs in private enterprises, which directly affects the further development of the private sector. Labor contract is the legal basis for establishing labor relations and defining the rights and obligations of both parties. However, it is understood that the identification rate of the labor contracts of private enterprises in China is less than 20 percent, and many contracts are not standardized and also include unfair terms (Li, 2015). Some private enterprises tend to use this means to lower wages. For example, employees get paid for their piecework during overtime working hours. The payment is calculated based on the effective working hours, which is much lower than the statutory minimum level. Moreover, it is still quite common that in many remote or underdeveloped regions, enterprises pay salaries in arrears or depress the contracted wages (Li, 2014).

## Conclusion

The development of the market economy in China creates good conditions for private enterprises. In recent years, the GDP contributed by the private economic components grew greatly. A large number of strong, large-scale and well-known private enterprises have emerged in the international market. At the same time, the growing strength and increasing market competitiveness motivate private enterprises to consider how to join the international competition, meet new challenges, and seek new development opportunities. However, due to the inherent deficiencies of private enterprises, many social problems have been increasingly exposed during their business development, as discussed in this chapter. According to observations, for many domestic well-known private enterprises, their achievement in sustainable development is closely related to their conscious fulfillment of their social responsibility duties (Xu et al., 2011). When market competition intensifies, sustainable development becomes a common concern for many enterprises in which social responsibility is placed as the top priority. In the following chapters, the actual CSR performance and trend of private enterprises will be further explored and discussed based on content analysis and other empirical studies.

## Notes

1 Data obtained from the National Bureau of Statistics of China, updated to December 31, 2015, available at data.stats.gov.cn/.
2 The "reform and opening up" policy was a strategic decision on "internal reform and opening to the outside world." It was put forward by the Third Plenary Session of the 11th Central Committee of the Communist Party of China in 1978. It was the first basic national policy since the establishment of the People's Republic of China. This decision led China's economy to enter into a period of rapid development.
3 Deng Xiaoping was a Chinese revolutionary and statesman. He was the paramount leader of the People's Republic of China from 1978 until his retirement in 1989.
4 Report of the 15th Central Committee of the Communist Party of China is available at language.chinadaily.com.cn/news/2013–2011/26/content_17132209.htm.
5 Reports of the 16th, 17th, and 18th Central Committee of the Communist Party of China are available at cpc.people.com.cn/GB/64162/64168/index.html.
6 2014 survey report of Chinese private enterprises, available at finance.sina.com.cn/nz/pr/.
7 Information is available at www.cspgp.org.cn/publicfiles/business/htmlfiles/cspgp/index.html.
8 News from www.tcxfw.gov.cn/Info/5102.aspx.
9 Article from the China Institute of Strategy and Management, available at www.cssm.org.cn/view.php?id=11860.
10 News from Sohu, available at news.sohu.com/57/54/news207105457.shtml.
11 News from Eastday, available at ej.eastday.com/eastday/train/node42813/node206641/node206648/u1a2913375.html.
12 Patent Law is available at www.sipo.gov.cn/zcfg/flfg/zl/fl/201509/t20150902_1169595.html.
13 Trademark Law is available at sbj.saic.gov.cn/flfg1/flfg/201309/t20130903_137807.html.
14 Zheng Baiwen company in its annual report disclosed the following: in 1994, the company's net profit was RMB 25.13 million; in 1995, their profit increased to RMB 27.4 million. After investigation, it was noted that the company used unethical measures to adjust their earnings, such as virtual rebate, understatement of cost and so on. Detailed information is available at finance.qq.com/zt2010/zbw/.
15 Yin Guangxia company produced fictitious financial statements and bribed external auditors to cover the facts for them. Their financial reports disclosed misleading information which caused significant losses to the investors. Detailed information is available at www.epochtimes.com/b5/1/8/2/n115541.htm.
16 Statistics from the Ministry of Environmental Protection of the People's Republic of China, available at datacenter.mep.gov.cn/index.

# 7 CSR reporting of private companies

## Introduction

In Western countries where the market economy system is well developed, a sound legal framework and market competition mechanism stimulate enterprises to fulfill their social responsibilities and disclose related information to the public (Liu et al., 2014). However, this kind of mechanism is currently inefficient in China during the economic transition period. There are more than 8 million private entities in China that account for over 70 percent of the capital market. For the creation of a good atmosphere of integrity management in the country, encouraging private companies to produce social reports is meaningful and helpful.

Although legal enforcement is not strong enough, many Chinese private enterprises voluntarily issue CSR reports to the public (Cui et al., 2015). In addition, private enterprises have made "significant contributions to the economy and have been more resilient in facing complicated situations and challenges than SOEs" (Zhang and Fung, 2006, p. 201). Many of them maintain long-term sustainable growth by credible operations and have shown large efforts in protecting the environment (Liu et al., 2014). Thus, the objective of this chapter is to investigate the motivation or extent of CSR information disclosure of private enterprises and their reporting practices.

## CSR reporting practices of private companies

Content analysis is conducted on 205 annual reports and 33 CSR reports issued by 61 private enterprises during 2006–2010. As shown in Table 7.1, a majority of the selected private enterprises did not issue standalone CSR reports or sustainability reports. Instead, a large amount of social information was disclosed in their annual reports and websites. To investigate the SAR practices of private companies, a similar approach was taken in the content analysis of SOEs that was applied in previous chapters.

*Table 7.1* Distribution of private enterprises, annual reports, and social reports

| Industry category | Industry name | Number of companies (Note 1) | Number of annual reports (2006–2010) | Number of standalone CSR reports and sustainability reports | | | | | |
|---|---|---|---|---|---|---|---|---|---|
| | | | | 2006 | 2007 | 2008 | 2009 | 2010 | Total |
| A | Agriculture, forestry, livestock farming and fishery | 3 | 15 | 0 | 0 | 1 | 1 | 0 | 2 |
| B | Mining | 6 | 15 | 0 | 0 | 1 | 2 | 1 | 4 |
| C-1 | Manufacturing (light) | 3 | 15 | 0 | 0 | 0 | 0 | 0 | 0 |
| C-2 | Manufacturing (heavy) | 3 | 15 | 0 | 0 | 0 | 1 | 1 | 2 |
| D | Electric power, gas, water production and supply | 4 | 15 | 0 | 0 | 0 | 1 | 1 | 2 |
| E | Construction | 5 | 15 | 0 | 0 | 1 | 0 | 0 | 1 |
| F | Transport and storage | 3 | 15 | 0 | 0 | 0 | 0 | 0 | 0 |
| G | Information Technology | 6 | 15 | 1 | 2 | 1 | 2 | 2 | 8 |
| H | Wholesale and retail trade | 6 | 15 | 0 | 0 | 1 | 2 | 2 | 5 |
| I | Finance and insurance | 2 | 10 | 0 | 1 | 1 | 1 | 1 | 4 |
| J | Real estate | 7 | 15 | 0 | 0 | 0 | 0 | 0 | 0 |
| K | Social service | 6 | 15 | 0 | 0 | 1 | 1 | 1 | 3 |
| L | Communication and Cultural Industry | 3 | 15 | 0 | 0 | 0 | 0 | 0 | 0 |
| M | Comprehensive | 4 | 15 | 0 | 0 | 1 | 1 | 0 | 2 |
| | Total | 61 | 205 | 1 | 3 | 8 | 12 | 9 | 33 |
| | Percentage of Total | 100% | 100% | 1.6% | 3% | 24% | 36% | 27% | 100% |

Note 1: Top three private companies ranked by capital size of each industry were selected for each fiscal year. As each year's ranking may be different due to the changes of capital size, a private enterprise selected in the former year may be off list in the later year and be replaced by a new one. Therefore, the total number of companies selected varied among industries. For Finance and Insurance industries, as most of the listed firms are SOEs, only two private enterprises were selected.

## Government forces

As shown in Figures 7.1 and 7.2, except the contents of financial performance and economic contribution, product quality and social events were the major CSR reporting aspects in the annual reports of private companies. Since 2008, the reporting of SO and PR information increased sharply. Presumably this was

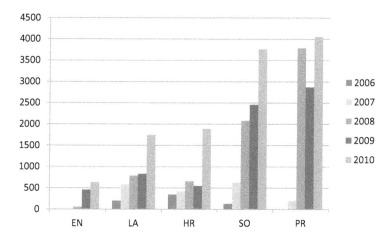

*Figure 7.1* Number of CSR key words disclosed in annual reports

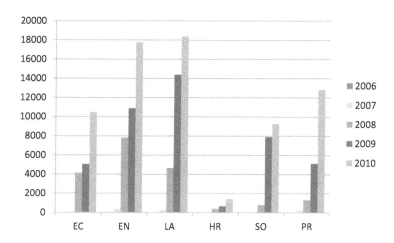

*Figure 7.2* Number of CSR key words disclosed in social reports

mainly stimulated by the serious industrial scandals and the various CSR policy documents issued during the year (see Appendix 2)

The 11th Five-Year Plan (www.gov.cn/ztzl/gmjj/), which supported the development of small and medium-sized enterprises, was implemented from 2006 onward. The state council conducted the second economic census in 2008, and the results showed that private enterprises were facing many problems and difficulties, such as high operating costs, financing difficulties, lack of human resources, low technical levels, and so on (www.stats.gov.cn). During the same year, the central government announced a number of policies aimed at stimulating private

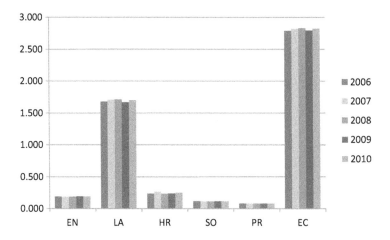

*Figure 7.3* Quality of CSR disclosure in annual reports

enterprises, such as tax benefits and technical support. Therefore, in order to earn more resources and to be viewed favorably by the government, CSR reporting became an effective means for creating a good image and building relationships with the policy makers. After all, the government is using the taxpayers' money to support their development. Resources are prioritized according to the social contribution made by the SOEs. While private companies were eager to show themselves positively through CSR reporting, they neglected training on standard CSR reporting methods; the layout and contents of their CSR reports are not standardized and lack references to international or domestic CSR reporting initiatives. This also explains why the quality of CSR disclosure in annual reports remains unchanged while the quantity showed an increasing trend during 2006–2010 (see Figures 7.1 and 7.3).

In March 2010, President Hu made an important speech mainly for the development of the non-state-owned economic sector (www.cppcc.gov.cn/zxww/shiyijiesanci/home/). He pointed out the important role of private companies with regard to CSR aspects and hoped that private companies could secure and improve the people's livelihood, enhance self-quality, and make a greater contribution to society. This speech further improved the private enterprises' confidence and became a driving force to stimulate their business development. Moreover, in late 2009, CASS published China's Corporate Social Responsibility Reporting Guidelines, which were considered as an official standard for private firms to prepare social reports. Furthermore, in 2010, the All-China Federation of Industry and Commerce and Peking University jointly released the CSR guideline system for private firms to enhance the integrity and ethics management of private enterprises. Referring to Figure 7.4, the effect of releasing these guidelines is clear. The overall reporting quality improved tremendously in 2010.

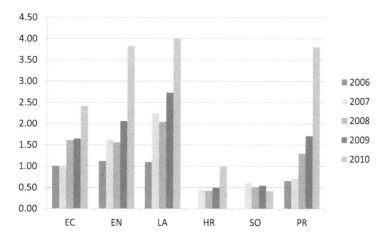

*Figure 7.4* Quality of CSR disclosure in social reports

## Overseas expansion need

In Figure 7.4, it can be seen that the reporting quality on environment (EN), labor (LA), and product quality (PR) showed substantial improvement. To investigate the rationale behind this change requires reference to the government policy. During the period of the 11th Five-Year Plan (2006–2010), while the Western world was facing another round of financial crisis, many private companies proactively entered the international market under the encouragement of the preferential "walking out" policy.[1] Their overseas investments were no longer restricted to Africa, Latin America, and other less-developed areas. Instead, they started to open up and generate businesses in Oceania, North America, Europe, Japan, and other developed regions or countries.[2] In addition, to meet domestic needs of sustainable growth in energy resources, some private enterprises began to acquire energy and mineral resources from overseas markets.[3] More importantly, the acquisition of world-leading or internationally well-known brands can help Chinese private enterprises to expand foreign markets, through bringing in advanced technology, modern managerial expertise, and qualified specialists.

According to the report issued by the National Bureau of Statistics (www. stats.gov.cn), in 2012, the private sector in China invested USD 25.5 billion in overseas mergers and acquisition projects of private companies, which was seven times the 2008 figure. The growth rate reached 600 percent during the past five years. To win a bid in foreign markets where CSR is a highly rated aspect, private enterprises could try to enhance their CSR performance, provide more detailed presentations of CSR information in the annual reports and CSR reports, and possibly highlighting these reports to gain maximum attention. CSR reports are the most important channel or medium for exhibiting companies' social performance to overseas and other potential stakeholders. Thus, to ensure sustainable development, private enterprises began to explore a long-term investment model, rather than focusing only on the immediate return on investment by building brands or business images through the improvement on environment, labor, and product quality aspects.

## CSR disclosure on websites

To obtain a thorough picture of social reporting practices of private firms, CSR information on the websites of selected companies was also reviewed and analyzed. Overall, the information disclosed is general, descriptive, and without detailed explanations and statistics. The average quality scores of key CSR indicators are EC0.69, EN0.80, LA0.90, HR0.07, SO1.2, and PR0.71. As shown in Figure 7.5, the human resource dimension is nearly nonexistent and accounts for only two percent of the total disclosure volume and with very brief descriptions. This phenomenon is also identified in both the annual reports and the social reports. The primary cause is that most of the private enterprises do not have much to be reported. Lack of technical personnel and qualified staff is always a problem. In addition, they cannot afford the high costs of employee welfare and benefits. The second finding is that only 32 percent of the selected companies placed a CSR page on their websites. The rest of them only disclosed social information in the relevant company news, investor relations, company profiles, and similar pages. Moreover, 10 percent of the companies did not have any CSR communication channel for stakeholders; 37 percent of them provided more than one communication methods, and only four or five out of 205 enterprises set Bulletin Board Systems or blogs for open discussions of their CSR issues.

All in all, the first impression provided is that CSR is not perceived as an important topic on the websites of most of the observed private companies. Competitive advantage, product functions, and innovation as well as investor relations occupied the major space on the screen. A possible reason behind this is that a growing number of private firms with global ambitions are expanding to Europe and North America. They are generally young and highly profit-driven. Many of them are high-tech oriented and emphasize continuous product innovation and after-sales service. To make good use of the most convenient and efficient media, namely, the internet and the World Wide Web, they are eager to promote their products to consumers and show off their competitive advantages or growth potential to investors rather than the CSR and social aspects of their companies.

## CSR weakness of private companies

Based on the content analysis of the reports and websites, a weakness of the private enterprises was identified that reflects their shallow understanding of the CSR concept and practice.

Many high-level managers in private enterprises do not have more than a superficial understanding of social responsibility. They still think CSR means

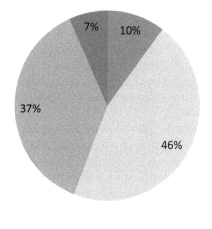

- A=no communication channel
- B=email address or message board or contact no.
- C=email address or message board and contact no.
- D=BBS

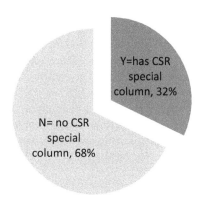

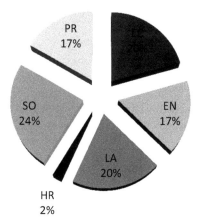

*Figure 7.5* Analysis of CSR disclosure on websites

doing good things in the community, giving donations, and so on. They fail to link CSR with the long-term development of society. In addition to the above findings through content analysis, the China Entrepreneurs Survey System also organized and implemented the "China Business Operator Questionnaire Survey" (www.ceoinchina.com/) in 2011 and obtained similar results. The results showed that private enterprises agree to fulfill their economic, legal, ethical, and public responsibilities. They most clearly recognized economic responsibility, which was followed by social welfare and cultural responsibilities. However, environmental responsibility had lower recognition.

The survey result also shows that although the awareness level of private enterprises in social welfare was lower than that of state-owned and foreign-funded enterprises, the degree of difference was not so obvious. Their awareness of economic responsibility reached 63 percent, which was higher than 60 percent of the observed foreign-invested enterprises. However, they were less aware of the other major CSR dimensions compared to the other two forms of businesses, especially in the environment aspect. Their level of understanding in that area was even less than 15 percent, far below that of state-owned enterprises (40 percent) and foreign-invested companies (41 percent). This shows that private enterprises pay much more attention to short-term economic benefit and focus on social responsibilities that are easy to produce quick social impacts. There appears to be a lack of understanding by the private sector of those social responsibilities with longer payback periods. For example, the donation to sales ratio of private companies was 0.43 percent, which was much higher than that of foreign companies and similar to the level of SOEs. However, their investment in environmental protection only accounted for 0.41 percent of their sales figure, which was far below that of SOEs (0.91 percent) and foreign-invested companies (0.61 percent).

## Conclusion

After the reform and opening up, with the development of the market economy, Chinese private enterprises have gone from strength to strength. Up to the end of 2010, the number of registered private enterprises exceeded 8.4 million, accounting for 74 percent of the total number of companies in China (www.stats.gov. cn). It is undeniable that the private economic sector has become an indispensable part of China's economy. Furthermore, with rapid overseas expansion and investments, private companies have also become an important player in the global market. Therefore, CSR reporting of the private sector is extremely important for building up a harmonious society and a good image of products made in China. In the process of creating a sound CSR environment, the government plays an active role in encouraging, guiding, and driving the development of social reporting of private companies.

## Notes

1 The CCP today has adopted and expanded Deng's 'open door' policies, encouraging foreign investment by 'inviting in'(*qingjinlai* 請進來) overseas enterprises and has

promoted the 'walking out' (*zouchuqu* 走出去) of Chinese firms into international markets, as well as the development of the commodity and service industries' capability to compete globally (Shi, 2001).

2 News from Sohu Finance dated January 4, 2013, available at business.sohu.com/20130104/n362318121.shtml.

3 News from Guangzhou Municipal Commission of Commerce dated October 21, 2009, available at www.gzcoc.gov.cn/article.jsp?columnId=2c9081ee2cbf9809012cc030568d038e&id=29960.

# 8    Development of foreign-invested companies in China

## Introduction

The tide of globalization has had a profound impact on the businesses of the world, including multinational companies. To adapt to the trend of economic integration, multinational companies have begun to adjust their business strategies and have significantly accelerated the speed and scale of production. These firms play a pivotal role in the development of the world economy.

China began to open to the outside world in the early 1980s. Many foreign direct investments were attracted, and thus new companies have been formed in China. These companies are mainly of three types: Sino-foreign equity joint venture,[1] Chinese-foreign cooperative enterprises,[2] and wholly foreign-owned enterprises.[3] The general name given to these enterprises in China is "foreign-invested companies." From 1978, the early stage of the reform, and the opening up, until 1991, the forms of foreign direct investment were mainly Sino-foreign joint ventures and Sino-foreign corporations. Among them, Sino-foreign joint ventures had a dominant position; their investment accounted for 50.8 percent of total utilized investment value in China and reached its peak in 1991 (Gao, M. et al., 2005). The share of wholly foreign-owned enterprises at this stage was very small and extremely unstable. Since 1992, the proportion of wholly foreign-owned enterprises began to rise substantially, from 27.1 to 75.5 percent in 2015 (see Appendix 8), while the proportion of Sino-foreign joint ventures in 1992 reached its peak, followed by a significant decline. The proportion decreased from 50.8 percent to around 20.5 percent in 2015 (see Appendix 8). The share of Chinese-foreign cooperative enterprises had remained at about 20 percent for a long period during the 1990s (Gao et al., 2008), followed by a sharp drop after the year 1998 and decreased to 1.5 percent by 2015 (see Appendix 8).

After 2001, the investment approach of foreign direct capital has undergone substantial changes. Since 1998, the proportion of wholly foreign-owned enterprises has exceeded that of the Sino-foreign joint ventures and has become a major foreign capital utilization method in China. After that, the number of wholly foreign-owned enterprises grew faster than other types of enterprises; with the total number accounting for 65.5 percent of all foreign-funded enterprises in 2013 (Xu, 2013).

For 2013, the total assets of the secondary and tertiary industry foreign-funded enterprises amounted to USD 138 billion, of which the proportion of the secondary industry was 58.70 percent and the proportion of the tertiary industry was 41.30 percent. In terms of the number of corporate units, employees, and the total amount of assets, the secondary industry still remained at the top place, while the proportion of the tertiary industry continued to increase at the same time (Xu, 2013). Many service industries (e.g., real estate, leasing and business services, wholesale and retail trade, transportation, warehousing and postal services, information transmission, computer services and the software industry) showed an upward trend. The largest increase was in the real estate industry, up to 28.96 percent in 2014 (from 2004). In 2014, the financial industry, the scientific research and technical services industry, and the geological prospecting industry jumped to the top sixth and seventh positions among all the industries in terms of their total investments. Before that, none of them was on the list (Xu, 2016).

The above statistics have obviously reflected the significant changes in the foreign-invested sector, mainly in the capital structures and industry distributions. Apart from the economic impact during this transformational process, the sector has also had a dramatic influence on many aspects of Chinese culture and society. The following sections look in greater depth at the evolution process of foreign-invested companies and their CSR impacts in China.

## Evolution process

In the process of attracting foreign investments into China, the investment forms have also changed. When foreign investors first entered China, due to restrictions of investment policies and other reasons, most of them chose to form joint ventures or to cooperate with Chinese companies. However, in terms of actual operations, the cost of joint ventures was very high, and operations were inefficient. In the past two decades, there has been a tendency toward wholly foreign investments (see Appendix 8). Based on the statistics, the process adopted by multinational companies in China can be divided into the following three stages.

### The first stage: exploration period

The exploration period can be considered as running from the beginning of the reform and opening up to the year 1991. During this stage, the use of foreign direct investment in China was mainly in the forms of Sino-foreign joint ventures and Chinese-foreign cooperative enterprises, among which the market share of Sino-foreign joint ventures kept growing and reached its peak in 1991, as stated earlier. The share of wholly foreign-owned enterprises at this stage was very small and extremely unstable. During the early period of the reform and opening up, when the economic system was not perfect and opaque, the construction of domestic infrastructure was relatively backward and the overall investment environment was poor. Therefore, joint venture and cooperative enterprises with flexible investments had shorter cooperation periods, and less risky investment portfolios were more prevalent.

The characteristics of foreign investments in this period included the following factors. First, during this period not only was the investment growth rate relatively slow but the investment scale was relatively small as well. The sector mainly concentrated on labor-intensive processing industries, and the technical content was weak. Second, foreign investors in this period were extremely cautious. They made some tentative small-scale investments and took a wait-and-see attitude toward the development of China's market economy. Many of the businesses concentrated on packaging, mainly imported assembly works. Nevertheless, there were some multinational companies in China with relatively high starting points, such as Shanghai Bell Co., Ltd. (now Alcatel-Lucent Shanghai Bell Co., Ltd.). However, the number of this type of enterprise was very limited. These were mainly those enterprises that had businesses in the "old" China and later returned to the market for further investment. For example, Siemens had opened a representative office in Beijing in 1982. Third, the investors were mainly Hong Kong, Macau, and overseas Chinese. Finally, the investments of large multinational companies in China were very limited, and their projects lacked systematic mechanisms. In the 1980s, the foreign direct investment made by multinational corporations in China was strictly considered as international trade behavior rather than productive investment behavior. During that period, the investment motivations of foreign-invested companies focused more on office establishment, opening marketing outlets, and collection of China's investment policy information and market information.

### The second stage: transition period

At the beginning of 1992, Deng Xiaoping inspected South China and delivered an important speech. This speech has been treated as a major ideological emancipation in the course of China's reform and development. It has promoted not only the pace of China's socialist market economy but also the emphasis on the major changes in using foreign investment policies in China. During this period, China made further amendments and improvements in major laws and policies involving foreign investment. For example, in 1990, the Law on Sino-foreign Equity Joint Ventures was amended. In 1995, the State Planning Commission, the Economic and Trade Commission, and the Ministry of Foreign Trade and Economic Cooperation jointly issued the "Guide to Foreign Investment" and the "Catalog of Foreign Investment Industries." In 2000, the government amended the Law on Sino-Foreign Contractual Joint Ventures" and "Law on Foreign Capital Enterprises. Additionally, six cities along the Yangtze River, 13 inland border cities, and 18 inland capital cities, were further opened up, which indicated the formation of a new pattern for opening to the outside world. As a result, the proportion of wholly foreign-owned enterprises has begun to rise considerably since 1992 (see Appendix 8), while the proportion of Sino-foreign joint ventures has shown a downward trend after reaching its peak in 1992. The share of Chinese and foreign cooperative enterprises remained at about 20 percent until 1998.

Foreign investment in this period included the following characteristics. The number and the scale of foreign investments were significantly different than those during the previous stage. The total investment amount during this period (1992–1998) accounted for around 14 times that of the last period (see Appendix 8). In addition, the investment amount of individual projects made by multinational companies had also increased gradually, and the relevance among projects invested in by the same company increased as well. Management and technical skills improved a great deal. At this stage, large multinational companies had gradually become the leading foreign investors in China. Until 1998, 400 out of the world's 500 largest multinational companies had made investments in China. The industries were mostly dominated by the productive and manufacturing sectors.

### The third stage: development period

The form of foreign direct investment in China has undergone significant changes since 1998. The number of wholly foreign-owned enterprises exceeded for the first time that of the Sino-foreign joint ventures and became China's major foreign investment. Since then, the proportion of wholly foreign-owned enterprises has been increasing rapidly, from 41.9 percent in 1998 to 77.17 percent in 2005, which was much higher than the share of Sino-foreign joint ventures and Chinese-foreign cooperative enterprises. Most multinational companies in China now are wholly foreign-owned businesses. With the rapid and stable development of the Chinese economy, the confidence of foreign investors in China has also gradually increased. Their motive has also changed significantly. Their fields of investment expanded to the tertiary industries and covered a wide range of service sectors.

The year 2001 was another turning point for China's reform and opening up. Major changes in foreign investment policies were implemented during this critical year. China successfully joined the WTO in 2001. On the one hand, joining the WTO provided a platform for domestic enterprises to compete in the international market; on the other hand, joining the WTO forced China to adapt to the new rules of international competition. The government has made new adjustments and amendments to the investment policies and laws of multinational corporations in China, so that the competition between foreign investors and domestic enterprises tended to be equal. The Chinese legislature had revised the "Law on Sino-foreign Joint Ventures," the "Law on Chinese-foreign Cooperative Enterprises," the "Law on Foreign Enterprises and the Detailed Rules for enforcing the Regulations." In addition, in order to adapt to different foreign investment forms, in 2002 the related government authorities had introduced three other important policy documents: (1) "Notice of China Securities Regulatory Commission, the Ministry of Finance and the State Economic and Trade Commission on the Relevant Issues concerning the Transfer of State-Owned Shares and Corporate Shares of Listed Companies to Foreign Investors," (2)"Measures for the Administration of Securities Investment within the Borders of China by Qualified Foreign Institutional Investors," and (3) "Interim Provisions on Restructuring State-owned Enterprises with Foreign Investment." At the end of the same year, the government issued the "Notice concerning the Relevant Issues on Strengthening the Approval, Registration, Foreign Exchange Control and Taxation Administration of Foreign-funded Enterprises" and made specific provisions on the relevant examination and approval procedures as well as the payment term of foreign investments.

Due to further improvements in the legal and institutional environment, the scale of foreign capital in China had expanded dramatically, and China's attraction towards foreign investors had also been reinforced. As a result, China replaced the United States as the country having the world's largest total amount of foreign investments. Compared to the previous stages, the motivations of foreign-invested companies have undergone a marked change; their major business objectives have turned out to be "to open up the Chinese market" and "to establish the production base in China." Furthermore, the emphasis on cheap raw materials in China had been greatly reduced. Only around 16 percent of the subsidiaries in China still focused on low-cost production. This shows that during the new historical period, multinational companies in China have experienced great changes in their investment strategy and have gradually turned to an in-depth integration strategy (*China Statistical Yearbook, 2016*).

## CSR impacts

### *Stimulating improvement of technology and enhancing scientific research and development capabilities in China*

With the improvement of the investment environment in China, an increasing number of foreign-invested enterprises have desired to win a place in the Chinese market. To this end, the competition between these foreign companies became increasingly fierce. They moved their research and development centers to China in order to improve their competitiveness, seize market opportunities, integrate their scientific research with production strategies, and finally, to better meet the needs of Chinese consumers and generate higher profits. According to the statistics from the Ministry of Commerce (www.mofcom.gov.cn/), in 2001 China signed a total number of 3,900 contracts with foreign investors for the acquisition of technology. The total contracted amount was around USD 9.09 billion, out of which technical costs constituted USD 4.4 billion, accounting for 48.3 percent of the total. In 2013, the number of technical contracts signed reached 12,448. The total amount (USD 43.36 billion) was almost 10 times the total in 2001, of which technical expenditures accounted for 94.8 percent of the total contract amount.

Foreign-invested enterprises occupy an important position in China in terms of the number of companies, the population of employees, the investment in human resources, and funding of research and development. They also stand out with respect to the number of projects for developing new products, expenditures, sales revenue, and the number of effective invention patents (see Table 8.1). Their research and development activities made a significant positive impact on technology introduction and innovation. They also created a spillover effect on China's technological progress through imports of equipment, setting up of research and development centers in China, technology extensions of product chains, provision of technical assistance to collaborative enterprises, personnel training, and so on.

In summary, there are three major positive impacts of foreign investments on scientific research and development in China. First, foreign investors brought innovative ideas and thinking to Chinese firms, which were originally considered as the main weaknesses of domestic companies. Although many Chinese enterprises now have R&D departments, the real research activities accounted for only about 30 percent (www.mofcom.gov.cn/). They would rather put a lot of money and manpower in advertising than in technological innovations and inventions. The arrival of foreign R&D institutions in China not only helped Chinese enterprises to realize the importance of technology and research but also enabled them to cultivate their own innovative thinking and ideas.

Second, Chinese enterprises have started to realize the importance of R&D management. At present, the domestic R&D institutions can only be regarded as "invention centers," lacking fitness and integration with their own organizations. The reason for this is that very few companies have established rigorous research and development systems. There is a lack of relevant management skills. In a sense, all R&D activities should be incorporated into the operation and management of the entire organization, making innovation management serve the production and decision-making processes as well as the marketing strategies of the company.

Third, foreign investors also help to change the tradition of indoor research in Chinese industries. Many multinational companies and universities carry out

*Table 8.1* Foreign investments in high-tech industry

| Statistic items | 2014 |
| --- | --- |
| Number of enterprises | 4479 |
| Number of employees | 3,772,000 |
| Revenue of main business (in billion US dollars) | $652.4 |
| Total profit (in billion US dollars) | $26.4 |
| Number of enterprises with research and development activities | 1513 |
| Number of research and development personnel | 151,478 |
| Expenditure on research and development (in billion US dollars) | $4,870 |
| Number of projects for developing new products | 13,126 |
| Expenditure on developing new products (in billion US dollars) | $6.4 |
| Sales revenue of new products (in billion US dollars) | $147 |
| Number of valid invention patents | 26,836 |

Source: China Statistics Yearbook on High Technology Industry

various forms of cooperation, including establishment of scholarships, donation of equipment, commissioned research, and the establishment of cooperative R&D institutions. Colleges and universities are also willing to cooperate with multinational companies to support their own scientific research, to teach, and to enable them to access state-of-the-art scientific or technical knowledge. Some Chinese universities and foreign researchers in China have established long-term cooperation. Among the foreign-funded research institutions, more than 30 percent have cooperated with universities or other domestic research institutions in China. This form of cooperation provides a platform for the development of scientific research in China, and universities can transform their research achievements into practical productivity and create incentive mechanisms for future researches. Additionally, a good platform can be built for students to apply the knowledge they have acquired into actual practices and also contribute to the development of advanced scientific research personnel.

### Making significant economic contributions

The economic contributions made by foreign-invested companies can be reflected in terms of two aspects: (1) their GDP proportion and increment in the national economy, and (2) their influence in the development of foreign trade in China.

During 1979–2015, China's actual utilization of foreign capital amounted to USD 1642.3 billion and became the highest among developing countries. Table 8.2 shows the weight of foreign direct investment in the national economy.

For the second aspect, the import and export of foreign-invested enterprises is an important driving force for the growth of China's foreign trade. According to Table 8.3, in 1985, the import and export volume of foreign-invested enterprises was only USD 3 billion, accounting for 4.5 percent of the total trade volume in the year. In 2006, it increased to USD 1,036.4 billion, accounting for nearly 60 percent of the total national import and export amount. In addition, foreign

*Table 8.2* Weight of foreign direct investment (FDI) in the national economy (percent)

| Year | FDI/GDP | FDI/Investment in fixed assets | Weight of FDI industrial output in GDP |
|------|---------|--------------------------------|----------------------------------------|
| 1985 | 0.64 | 2.26 | – |
| 1995 | 0.52 | 15.65 | – |
| 2006 | 2.32 | 4.77 | 20.98 |
| 2007 | 2.14 | 4.14 | 21.05 |
| 2008 | 1.96 | 3.71 | 19.48 |
| 2009 | 1.85 | 2.74 | 18.42 |
| 2010 | 1.8 | 2.84 | 17.91 |
| 2011 | 1.41 | 2.41 | 16.80 |
| 2012 | 1.53 | 1.88 | 15.32 |
| 2013 | 1.24 | 1.63 | 14.96 |
| 2014 | 1.16 | 1.43 | 14.28 |

Source: Ministry of Commerce and National Bureau of Statistics

*Table 8.3* Import and export of foreign-invested companies (% billion US dollars)

| Year | Total import and export of foreign-invested companies | Total import and export of the country | Weight |
|---|---|---|---|
| 1985 | 3.0 | 73.9 | 4.05 |
| 2000 | 236.7 | 474.3 | 49.91 |
| 2005 | 831.7 | 1422.1 | 58.48 |
| 2006 | 1036.4 | 1760.6 | 58.87 |
| 2007 | 1256.8 | 2174.4 | 57.80 |
| 2008 | 1410.5 | 2561.6 | 55.06 |
| 2009 | 1217.4 | 2207.2 | 55.16 |
| 2010 | 1600.3 | 2972.8 | 53.83 |
| 2011 | 1860.1 | 3641.9 | 51.07 |
| 2012 | 1893.9 | 3867.5 | 48.97 |
| 2013 | 1919.1 | 4160.3 | 46.13 |
| 2014 | 1984.0 | 4303.0 | 46.11 |
| 2015 | 1834.6 | 3958.6 | 46.34 |

Source: China External Economic Statistical Yearbook 2016

investment has led to the rapid development of processing trade. The development and expansion of processing trade is the first form of foreign capital utilized since the 1980s. In the 1990s, foreign investment entered into China's manufacturing industries in a concentrated manner, encompassing the automobile, machine manufacturing, computers, telecommunications, equipment manufacturing, and electronics industries. During the initial stage of investment, a large number of imports was required for the assembly of spare parts, machinery, and equipment. These goods were then exported to overseas markets after assembly. With the strengthening of China's manufacturing industry, multinational companies gradually expanded into China's upstream and downstream value-chain industry and completed the industrial gradient transfer. Furthermore, foreign investors moved more R&D, sales, and other departments to China. This has not only helped China to transit its industrial structure from a labor-intensive mode to a capital and technology-intensive mode but has enhanced the level of China's export-oriented economy.

### Facilitating the exchange and introduction of talent

Foreign investments can bring the technology spillover effect back to the host country, not only for promoting technological progress and industrial upgrading but also for bringing more training and enhancing human resource mobility. Since the beginning of the 21st century, the training of local employees in foreign-invested enterprises has become an important foundation for technology spillovers, and the flow of talent between foreign-invested enterprises and domestic enterprises is considered to be an important channel for training.

As market competition in China has become sharper, foreign-invested enterprises pay an increasing amount of attention to the role of R&D activities in technological innovation. Therefore, the proportion of funds and human resources invested in R&D activities has increased significantly and more and more technical personnel have been trained. In addition, the entry of foreign capital itself also brought in some foreign talent, such as management and technical personnel. The introduction of this foreign talent has played a positive role in promoting domestic and international personnel exchange as well as imparting advanced management experience and technical knowledge.

## Conclusion

In summary, the CSR contribution made by foreign-invested companies are mainly in terms of the economy, technology improvements, and employment and training of human resources. Overall, this chapter serves as an introduction to the role of foreign-invested companies from the perspectives of their historical development and CSR contribution in China, which will bring further insights for understanding their CSR performance to be examined in the upcoming chapters.

## Notes

1 According to Article 4 of the "Law on Sino-Foreign Equity Joint Ventures" (SFEJV), a SFEJV is defined as "a limited liability company, the proportion of investment contributed by a foreign partner as its share of the registered capital of an equity joint venture shall in general be no less than 25 per cent." (Available at english.mofcom.gov.cn/article/lawsdata/chineselaw/200301/20030100062855.shtml).

2 According to Article 1 of the "Law on Chinese-foreign cooperative enterprises" (CFCE), the objective in establishing CFCE is to "expand economic cooperation and technological exchanges with other countries." The Law is formulated to "help foreign enterprises and other economic organizations or individuals to establish CFCE in China with Chinese enterprises or other economic organizations in accordance with the principle of equality and mutual benefit." (Available at english.mofcom.gov.cn/aarticle/policyrelease/internationalpolicy/200705/20070504715781.html).

3 According to Article 2 of the "Law on Wholly Foreign-Owned Enterprises" (WFOE), WFOE are "enterprises with sole foreign investment and established within Chinese territory, . . . with their capital provided totally by a foreign investor. It does not include branches in China of foreign enterprises or other economic organizations." (Available at english.mofcom.gov.cn/aarticle/lawsdata/chineselaw/200301/20030100062858.html).

# 9 CSR reporting of foreign-invested companies in China

## Overview

In 2005, the Chinese Academy of International Trade and Economic Cooperation (CAITEC) of the Ministry of Commerce released a report on CSR performance of multinational enterprises in China (Report on Multinational Companies [MNCs] in China 2005).[1] It indicated that foreign companies have brought a lot of benefits to the local market, such as technology, modern corporate governance methods, and investment. More importantly, they also introduced advanced concepts and practices of social and environmental responsibilities to Chinese society.

However, the report also mentioned that a number of MNCs have acted immorally and were in violation of CSR principles. For example, several well-known companies were exposed for their food quality and safety problems, such as the "Sudan" event, excessive iodine in milk powder, and price fraud in supermarkets. Some other firms reduced employees' salary casually and forced them to work overtime. These enterprises do not have labor unions, and employees cannot claim their rights when they are fired without justification. Other problems like bribery, evading taxes illegally, and market monopoly have also brought negative impacts on the image of MNCs in China.[2] Therefore, understanding and investigating the social reporting level and the trend of foreign companies in China is important for the government in order to regulate MNCs' activities and to promote sustainable economic and social development in China.

This chapter reviews and analyzes the CSR information disclosed in 120 annual reports and 97 social reports of the largest foreign-invested companies in China. These companies are mainly from labor intensive industries and have significant environmental impact due to their manufacturing processes, such as electronics manufacturing, and automobile and chemical companies, notwithstanding that the statistics by the Ministry of Commerce in 2010 (www.yearbook.org.cn) indicated the proportion of foreign-invested companies in agriculture, forestry, livestock farming and fishery industries, and real estate weighed nearly 10 percent in China. In the list of the top 500 foreign investors in China (the base document of sample selection), no standalone CSR reports or annual reports related to China operation were released from 2006 to 2010 by these companies. As shown in Table 9.1, the number of CSR or sustainability reports of the observed firms increased from eight in 2006 to 51 in 2010. Reports issued by Japanese and US companies account for large percentages, which occupied 40 percent and 19 percent, respectively. European firms are also active in CSR reporting. Their social reports account for 12 percent of the total observations.

In terms of reporting frequency, 60 percent of the observed companies issued CSR reports in more than three consecutive years; and 34 percent issued reports every year during the observed period. These indicate that CSR reporting of the selected foreign-invested companies have good continuity. From the perspective

*Table 9.1* Distribution of foreign enterprises (MNCs), annual reports, and social reports

| Industry category | Industry name | Number of companies | Number of annual reports (2006–2010) | Number of CSR reports and sustainability reports | | | | | |
|---|---|---|---|---|---|---|---|---|---|
| | | | | 2006 | 2007 | 2008 | 2009 | 2010 | Total |
| A | Agriculture, forestry, livestock farming and fishery | 0 | 0 | 0 | 0 | 0 | 0 | 0 | 0 |
| B | Mining | 3 | 15 | 0 | 0 | 1 | 3 | 3 | 7 |
| C-1 | Manufacturing (light) | 9 | 15 | 2 | 2 | 3 | 4 | 5 | 16 |
| C-2 | Manufacturing (heavy) | 8 | 15 | 2 | 3 | 3 | 5 | 5 | 18 |
| D | Electric power, gas, water production and supply | 0 | 0 | 0 | 0 | 0 | 0 | 0 | 0 |
| E | Construction | 3 | 15 | 0 | 0 | 1 | 3 | 3 | 7 |
| F | Transport and storage | 3 | 15 | 0 | 0 | 3 | 4 | 5 | 12 |
| G | Information Technology | 12 | 15 | 1 | 1 | 3 | 3 | 4 | 12 |
| H | Wholesale and retail trade | 6 | 15 | 1 | 0 | 3 | 5 | 6 | 15 |
| I | Finance and insurance | 0 | 0 | 0 | 0 | 0 | 0 | 0 | 0 |
| J | Real estate | 0 | 0 | 0 | 0 | 0 | 0 | 0 | 0 |
| K | Social service | 0 | 0 | 0 | 0 | 0 | 0 | 0 | 0 |
| L | Communication and Cultural Industry | 0 | 0 | 0 | 0 | 0 | 0 | 0 | 0 |
| M | Comprehensive | 15 | 15 | 0 | 1 | 3 | 3 | 3 | 10 |
| | Total | 59 | 120 | 6 | 7 | 20 | 30 | 34 | 97 |
| | Percentage of Total | 100% | 100% | 6% | 7% | 21% | 31% | 35% | 100% |

of reporting length, most of the CSR or sustainability reports exceed 30 pages. Reports of more than 50 pages account for 35 percent, and those with less than 10 pages were 2.4 percent of the total sample. For the reporting format, "sustainability report" and "CSR report" weighed 83 percent and 10 percent, respectively. Sixteen percent of the companies released more than one type of social report. Apart from CSR or sustainability reports, they also released "environmental information reports" or "environment, health and safety reports."

## Reporting quantity and quality

### *Reporting quantity*

Referring to Chapter 1, CSR has been growing rapidly in China since 2006. An increasing number of Chinese enterprises have begun to realize the significance of the concept. The total number of CSR reports increased sharply since 2008. A similar increasing trend is identified in the CSR disclosure quantity of the observed foreign companies (see Figures 9.1 *and* 9.2). The years 2008 and 2009 were two critical years in the reporting of foreign companies with respect to CSR. During those years, the companies greatly increased the CSR content in their reports, especially in the areas of the environment, labor, and product quality. This was mainly due to several serious environmental and industrial scandals as well as some important instructions and policy documents issued by the Chinese government during that time.

In 2008, scandals concerning banned additives in pork, dyed buns, and hormone-injected watermelons were revealed, not to mention the notorious melamine-tainted dairy products that killed six children.[3] The number and severity of the tainted-food concerns had raised food safety to a controversial and critical

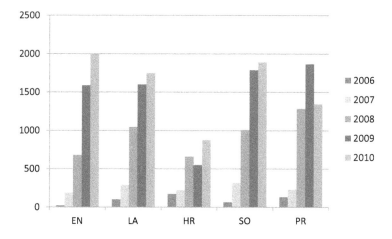

*Figure 9.1* Number of CSR key words in annual reports

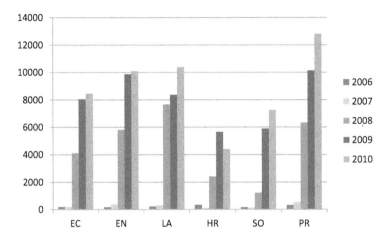

*Figure 9.2* Number of CSR key words in social reports

level in China. In addition, in the following year, a Japanese automobile manufacturer called back problematic cars.[4] A vendor was found selling expired food
products in foreign-invested supermarkets, and these were all reported by the
mass media.[5] Such events have stimulated foreign firms to closely scrutinize their
product quality following increased government vigilance and public concerns.
Correspondingly, in the annual reports and social reports, product quality contents have increased greatly since 2008 compared to prior years. Companies
started to provide more information concerning suppliers, product design and
development, and quality control procedures as well as the chemical ingredients
used (food industry).

Labor problems also drew much attention from the government and society in
China during that period. Key words such as "sweatshop," "labor suicides," and
"salaries in arrears" frequently appeared in the mass media. On the one hand,
given the rapid business expansion in China, foreign companies put much pressure on their employees and required them to work with higher efficiency. On the
other hand, Chinese white collar workers were no longer satisfied with working
in foreign-invested companies. They were eager for a middle-class life and to
safeguard their rights under the law. According to statistics, the number of labor
disputes that took place in foreign-invested companies increased by 55.6 percent in 2007.[6] In July 2007, the 28th session of the Standing Committee of the
Tenth National People's Congress passed the revised Labor Contract Law, which
became effective from January 1, 2008 onward.[7] The new labor law stimulated
legal consciousness in the labor market, provided more protection of labor rights
and interests, and clarified the obligations of employers. After the promulgation
of the law, labor welfare and benefits have become one of the major topics in
foreign companies' public reports.

The new labor law also emphasizes environment, health, and safety (EHS) issues, which were expected to be the top priorities for companies. A majority of the observed foreign companies have paid greater attention to these issues, made improvements in their supply chains, and improved CSR training. Furthermore, some foreign companies have established solid philanthropic programs involving environmental protection, community improvement, education enhancement, and agricultural development. Some even published special EHS reports to disclose issues such as employee exposure to poisonous materials as well as the frequency of significant incidents or major accidents. From another perspective, the improvement in environmental disclosure is also influenced by international treaties and the government's instructions. During the G8 Summit held in July 2008, by 2050 China has to commit to reduce its carbon dioxide emissions per unit of GDP by 50 percent.[8] As mentioned in many social reports, the headquarters of foreign companies delivered environmental protection objectives to their subsidiaries in China for responding to the call from the United Nations Framework Convention on Climate Change. In addition, the CAITEC issued the "Guidelines on Corporate Social Responsibility Compliance for Foreign Invested Enterprises in 2009."[9] The guidelines request foreign firms to adopt energy-saving technology and to establish reliable procedures for environmental emergencies. In the 2009 report, the disclosure of environmental issues responded well to the calls from the international community and Chinese government. Furthermore, disclosure on social aspects had also a sharp reinforcement in 2009. A number of annual reports and CSR reports of our observed firms provided a large quantity of information to explain how they have stressed the collaboration with local communities and responded and swiftly helped when a public emergency occurred. These are also important requirements mentioned by CAITEC in their guidelines.

### Reporting quality

In line with the trend of disclosure quantity, the quality of CSR reporting also significantly improved since 2008. However, in the annual reports the information was provided only generally, without much detail in the content. Although the environment, labor and safety dimensions relatively had higher rating, the disclosure quality was still far below the desired level (see Figure 9.3).

Comparatively speaking, most of the social reports have made progress in substance. Detailed descriptions, statistics, and figures were presented in a number of CSR reports analyzed in this study. Although the disclosure of Environment, Human Resource, Society and Product Quality have achieved continuous improvements and exceeded 3.5 points by 2010 (see Figure 9.4), the quality still has much room for improvement. The CSR report is an important communication channel between companies and their stakeholders. However, some MNCs did not provide enough information for different stakeholder groups. In addition, they did not respond promptly to some key issues or problems of concern to the public and their stakeholders. These reports are not likely to improve the

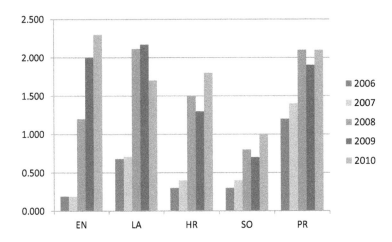

*Figure 9.3* Quality of CSR disclosure in annual reports

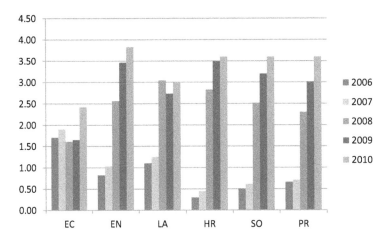

*Figure 9.4* Quality of CSR disclosure in social reports

firms' communication with society. Some other social reports merely mentioned the companies' regional operations and relevant policies or regulations in China without disclosing any quantitative data. Many failed to provide sufficient information on their social activities on the mainland. Compared with the global reports issued by parent companies, the regional reports lacked quantitative indicators. Some reports were even prepared under different standards. For example, qualitative descriptions of CSR policies, product innovation, and charity and donation constituted the major part of the content of many CSR reports issued specifically for the China market. On the other hand, key quantitative indicators of the China operations were absent or insufficient, such as the volume of energy consumption, water usage, waste air emissions, and waste water discharges. Another problem is that it is difficult to make longitudinal comparisons of the data disclosed since not much quantitative information was reported within consecutive years.

## Reporting incentives

Various forces drive the CSR reporting development of MNCs in China. On the one hand, foreign companies were under the pressures from Chinese society and international communities, as discussed earlier. Many MNCs moved their manufacturing and processing bases to China due to relatively cheap and rich labor resources. However, since 2007, with the enhancement of CSR awareness in Chinese society, many labor disputes, product quality, and pollution problems of foreign enterprises were exposed by the mass media. To maintain their business image, foreign companies issued social reports for their China operations and also integrated CSR information in their annual reports. Based on our content analysis, those topics were of great concern to the government and the public; EHS, labor and product quality, were largely covered in the reports.

On the other hand, CSR reporting can help foreign investors to build brand image and improve public relations. These companies aim to display their achievements through CSR reporting and delivering a friendly message to Chinese consumers and stakeholders in return for obtaining a good reputation in the market. For example, some Japanese companies disclosed their CSR activities of helping poor students and donations made to charitable institutions. One Japanese company even expressed understanding of the Japanese invasion against China during World War II and organized employees to watch movies with this theme.

Furthermore, the foreign-invested companies' production of social reports for the China market is also influenced by their parent companies and the CSR policies in their mother countries. From the headings of the reports, a majority of the Chinese enterprises used "CSR report" as the title. However, more than one-third of the observed foreign investors followed their parent companies to issue "sustainability reports," "environmental information reports," or "environment, health, and safety reports".

## Conclusion

In summary, the development of CSR reporting of foreign-invested companies in China has experienced its ups and downs. With abundant experiences in conducting CSR activities internationally, foreign investors provided valuable assistance in promoting CSR in the Chinese market, particularly in terms of internal operations. However, in the actual process of transplanting and implementing their global experiences to China, many issues and challenges emerged.

Poor understanding of the local culture and expectations have led to attempts to force-fit Western practices. The far-too-frequent emphasis on CSR as a public relations tool or to meet legal obligations has led to confusion and disappointment. There are no efficient incentives for foreign-invested companies to strive to be the best in the field, and local companies, in fact, can provide the impetus for the multinationals to act proactively in CSR.

## Notes

1 Xinhua news dated February 17, 2006, available at news.xinhuanet.com/fortune/200602/17/content_4190736.htm.
2 Legal Daily News dated November 15, 2011, available at www.chinanews.com/fz/2011/11-15/3459957.shtml.
3 2005–2010 major food safety scandals review, available at www.legaldaily.com.cn/zmbm/content/2010-03/04/content_2071821.htm?node=7574.
4 BBC news dated at October 10, 2012, available at www.bbc.com/news/business-19894322
5 China news dated at October 27, 2011, available at www.chinanews.com/life/2011/10-27/3417853.shtml.
6 *China Labor Statistical Year Book* 2008.
7 Official website of The National People's Congress of the P.R.C., available at www.npc.gov.cn/npc/xinwen/rdyw/hyhd/2007-07/20/content_369072.htm.
8 United Nations, Framework Convention on Climate Change, available at www.newsroom.unfccc.int.
9 CAITEC is an authority directly under the Ministry of Commerce. The introduction of this guideline is available at files.dlapiper.com/files/upload/Corporate_Social_Responsibility_compliance_by_foreign_invested_cos%20_in_PRC.pdf.

# 10  Triangulation

## Empirical study and interview analysis

## Introduction

In the previous chapters, the potential drivers of and management attitudes toward social reporting in China were discussed based on the content analysis results. Inferences about latent meanings of contents are permitted by using content analysis techniques, but they require triangulation and corroboration with independent evidence (Merton, 1968; Holsti, 1969; Heilman, 1976; Berg, 2008). Therefore, by incorporating the findings from the content analysis results (see Chapters 4, 7 and 9) with the literature (see Chapter 2), an empirical study and an interview analysis are presented in this chapter. By combining both qualitative and quantitative measures, the findings of this research can reliably address the main objective of this study, which is to explore and explain the CSR reporting motivations and practices of enterprises operating in China (see Chapter 1).

## Empirical study

In a developed market economic system (e.g., Western Europe and North America) where a more integrated institutional framework has been established, market competition and institutional requirements work together to push forward enterprises to fulfill their SAR responsibilities. In China, a similar mechanism is under development. The Chinese government becomes a key resource keeper and ultimately affects the business activities of companies (Han and Gan, 2013). According to Li et al. (2006), a political network (PN) has become an important strategic asset in a transitional economy. Enterprises establish a PN for resource allocation and management, which is a typical corporate political behavior. Therefore, in China, political relation is considered an effective alternative mechanism while the market economic system is still being established (Yu and Pan, 2008). In this circumstance, enterprises attempt to establish good relationships with the government, administrative organs, and other authorities by conducting more CSR activities and enhancing transparent SAR. Their major purpose is to obtain preferential treatment from the government so as to create competitive advantage for themselves in the market (Lin and Zhao, 2013). To verify the above phenomenon, a multiple regression model is composed to investigate the relationship between political relation and CSR reporting. This is an attempt to triangulate the previous content analysis results.

### Political relation and CSR reporting

In recent years, more and more enterprises proactively participate in politics. Many entrepreneurs have become National People's Congress (NPC) deputies and Chinese People's Political Consultative Conference (CPPCC) members (Li et al., 2006). In the special environment of China, setting up political connections may stimulate entrepreneurs to make response to the government's policies for sustainable development and for building a harmonious society. According to Porter and Kramer's analysis, taking up social responsibility is conducive to protecting the environment, easing social tensions, promoting social stability, and improving overall business environment. Entrepreneurs with consciousness of establishing strategic PNs are more likely to take this kind of interactive, win–win strategy (Porter and Kramer, 2006). In addition, under public scrutiny, politically related enterprises are more likely to take socially responsible actions that match their business image, such as proactively disclosing CSR information in response to policy documents issued by the government (Fan et al., 2007). Thus, the following hypothesis is posed.

H1: Companies with more political relations perform better in CSR reporting.

### Association relation and CSR reporting

Those entrepreneurs who failed to become NPC deputies, to become CPPCC members, or to obtain other political identities may establish and maintain political connections through participation in official or semi-official industrial associations and government related networks in order to gain some political and economic interests (Zhang and Zhang, 2005). In China, many industrial associations have close relationships with the central government, and some of them have even been formed by government authorities (Foster, 2011). Joining industrial associations can improve enterprises' business image and help them establish good PNs and accumulate more political capital for future development. Nevertheless, such benefits are always accompanied with responsibilities and obligations. These companies also have to face greater media and public exposure and pressure from the government and various stakeholder groups that encourage them to behave like socially responsible entities (Wu, 2005). Therefore, the second hypothesis is generated as follows.

H2: Companies with more association relations perform better in CSR reporting.

### SOEs and CSR reporting

Several studies have demonstrated that in order to build an ethical business environment, governments have developed a considerable number of social reporting initiatives that regulate CSR reporting practices of SOEs or government-linked companies (GLCs) (Garwin, 1983; Weidenbaum, 1999; Joseph, 2002). National governments have long been viewed as one of the most important agents that influence the behavior of enterprises by their defining and changing regulations, priorities, the landscape of reporting, and the "rules of the game" for companies. For example, Amran and Devi (2008) and Rahman et al. (2011) empirically investigated the influence of government on social reporting development and its impact on Malaysian GLCs. Therefore, in China, it is expected that SOEs are more willing to do CSR in order to meet their major shareholder's (the government) need, which is to promote CSR and create a good social reporting atmosphere. Hence hypothesis 3 is presented now.

H3: SOEs disclose more than private companies.

### Media attention and CSR reporting

Many researches have indicated that the degree of a company's media exposure is positively associated with its CSR disclosure (Bansal, 2005; Brammer and Pavelin, 2004; Bewley and Li, 2000; Cormier et al., 2004). In a study related to legitimacy theory, the role of mass media in exerting pressure on companies from the public is also discussed (Aerts and Cormier, 2009). Media exposure will increase public attention on a company's social performance and make it become the target of the supervisory authority (Bansal, 2005). According to Simon's (1992) research, the media are one of the major sources of environmental information. Additionally, empirical studies also find that the media have significant impact on corporate environmental responses (Bansal and Clelland, 2004; Bowen, 2000; Henriques and Sadorsky, 1996). Considering that environmental disclosure is a part of CSR reporting, the fourth hypothesis is proposed now.

H4: Media attention is positively associated with CSR reporting.

### Model

Based on the above discussions, a regression model is suggested below.

$$CSRD = \alpha + \beta1POL + \beta2ASSO + \beta3SOE + \beta4MED + \beta5BODSIZE + \beta6CON + \beta7LEV + \beta8SIZE + \beta9IND \text{ Dummy} + \varepsilon$$

Where
CSRD=Quality of CSR reporting;
POL=Political relation;
ASSO=Association relation;
SOE=State-owned enterprises;
MED=Media attention;
BODSIZE=Board size;
CON= Ownership concentration;

LEV= Leverage;
SIZE=Company size;
IND=Industry.

CSRD is measured by the RANKINS CSR report ratings (www.rksratings.com), which include the CSR ratings of all A-share companies in China. POL is a dummy variable to determine if any member of the board of directors is also in the position of NPC deputy or CPPCC member. A company is considered as having association relation (ASSO) if it has membership in any industrial association/NGO/CSR society, and the related information is collected from the company's annual report or official website. An observed enterprise is classified as a SOE if it is fully or partially owned by the government (Christiansen, 2011). The ownership data is extracted from CSMAR. For POL, ASSO, and SOE, if the answer is "yes," "1" is coded; if "no," "0" is recorded. MED is measured by the volume of news reported by the mass media and is manually collected via the internet.

Factors expected to have impact on CSRD are treated as control variables. Firms with good corporate governance structure usually have higher quality disclosure (Khan, 2010; Barkemeyer et al., 2015) Therefore, BODSIZE and CON are controlled in this research. The board size is measured by the number of directors. The ownership concentration is determined by the percentage of shares held by the top five shareholders (Liu et al., 2011; Johnson and Greening, 1999). Data of these two control variables are also extracted from CSMAR.

In addition, three variables commonly used in CSR studies are also controlled in the model. First, leverage is used as a proxy of financial risk (Belkaoui and Karpik, 1989; Brammer and Pavelin, 2008). Prior studies have shown a negative relationship between leverage and CSR reporting. For example, Brammer and Pavelin (2008) conclude that for companies with low leverage ratios, their managers will have less constraints on spending resources for CSR activities. Reverte (2009) points out that leverage is negatively correlated with CSR disclosure due to the pressures from creditors. Second, firm size is also adapted to and is positively associated with CSR disclosure (McWilliams and Siegel, 2000; Orlitzky, 2001). The third control variable is industry. According to prior studies, firms in industries that have greater potential impact on the environment are experience greater pressure with respect to environmental concerns than companies from less environmentally sensitive industries. These firms are more likely to disclose information related to environmental issues in order to enhance their corporate image (Hackston and Milne, 1996; Deegan and Gordon, 1996; Moneva and Llena, 2000; Campbell, 2003; Gao, S. et al., 2005; Cho and Patten, 2007; Brammer and Pavelin, 2008). Therefore, in this study, high-profile industries (e.g., mining, food and beverage, power, utility, steel, oil, and chemical) are coded as "1" and "0" is used to represent low-profile industries.

### Descriptive statistics

A-share companies listed in the Shanghai Stock Exchange from 2008–2013 were observed. Observations with missing data were deleted from the sample list. In addition, to eliminate the impact from outliers, variables of major interest were win-sorized by 1 percent, and finally, 2,927 firm-year observations are retained. As shown in Table 10.1, the overall SAR level of the selected firms is low, which is indicated by the mean value of 32.91. In addition, the standard deviation of 12.72 reveals that sample firms have substantial differences in SAR performance. Furthermore, based on the ownership type, SOEs account for 70 percent of the total sample size. Lower than expectation, the percentage of companies with political relations is 33 percent. However, 72 percent of these companies are members of a variety of associations. For media attention, on average six pieces of news related to a firm's CSR issues were reported annually. The maximum number of news reports is 64, and the minimum is zero. Overall, the variables of main interest are normally distributed, as no significant deviations between mean values and median values were identified.

## Univariate analysis

Table 10.2 presents the matrix of Pearson pair-wise correlations between the major variables. Consistent with expectation, political relations, association relations, and media attention are positively correlated ($p<0.001$; $p<0.05$) with CSR disclosure. The matrix also reflects that SOEs have a higher CSR reporting level compared to other types of enterprises. Although the conclusion made based on the univariate test might be overridden after controlling for other factors, the results have preliminarily verified hypotheses 1 to 4.

## Regression analysis

Table 10.3 presents the multiple regression results. In model (1), political relations are positively related to CSR disclosure at the 1 percent significance level.

*Table 10.1* Descriptive statistics of variables with main interest

| Variable | Min | Max | Mean | Median | Std dev |
|---|---|---|---|---|---|
| CSRD | 11.69 | 81.46 | 32.91 | 34.29 | 12.72 |
| POL | 0 | 1 | 0.33 | 0 | 0.47 |
| ASSO | 0 | 1 | 0.72 | 1 | 0.53 |
| SOE | 0 | 1 | 0.63 | 1 | 0.46 |
| MED | 0 | 64 | 6.36 | 8.00 | 5.28 |

*Table 10.2* Correlation matrix of variables with main interest

| | CSRD | POL | ASSO | SOE | MED |
|---|---|---|---|---|---|
| CSRD | 1 | | | | |
| POL | 0.441*** | 1 | | | |
| ASSO | 0.235** | −0.035 | 1 | | |
| SOE | 0.579*** | 0.187* | 0.097 | 1 | |
| MED | 0.289*** | 0.148* | 0.055 | 0.202** | 1 |

*,**,*** denote significance at the 10%, 5% and 1% levels, respectively.

*Table 10.3* Regression results

| Variables | Regression model | | | | |
|---|---|---|---|---|---|
| | *(1)* | *(2)* | *(3)* | *(4)* | *(5)* |
| POL | 4.750*** | | | | 3.483*** |
| ASSO | | 4.290*** | | | 2.290** |
| SOE | | | 3.335*** | | 1.984* |
| MED | | | | 3.274*** | 0.235 |
| BODSIZE | 1.420 | 5.672*** | 3.493 | 3.232* | 1.280 |
| CON | −0.013 | 0.059*** | 0.050* | 0.022 | 0.043* |
| LEV | −8.097* | −11.871*** | −11.534** | −7.343 | −5.328 |
| ROA | 8.749* | 3.954 | 5.365* | 7.382** | 6.389** |
| IND | 3.908*** | 1.736** | 3.657** | 3.239*** | 1.394* |
| SIZE | 0.983 | 0.876 | 1.252* | 0.738 | 0.057 |
| Intercept | −3.719** | 2.435** | 3.493*** | 2.584*** | 1.897* |
| Industry control | Yes | Yes | Yes | Yes | Yes |
| Adj–R square | 0.393 | 0.226 | 0.211 | 0.253 | 0.196 |
| P–value of difference | 0.000 | 0.000 | 0.000 | 0.000 | 0.000 |
| N | 2927 | 2927 | 2927 | 2927 | 2927 |

*,**,*** denote significance at the 10%, 5% and 1% levels, respectively

The result is in line with the research findings in previous chapters that show the existence of political relations can stimulate CSR reporting of enterprises in China. NPC/CPPCC membership is a part-time political duty. Directors elected as NPC/CPPCC members need to attend NPC/CPPCC meetings periodically and to relay the CSR instructions announced by the central government to their management team. Through this process, enterprises can better understand the CSR spirit introduced by the government and conduct better CSR reporting in response to the government's call.

The result of Model (2) also indicates a significant positive correlation between relation with associations and CSR disclosure. Companies having more memberships in industrial associations/NGOs/CSR societies perform better in CSR reporting. Many industrial associations and NGOs (such as China Banking Industry Association, China Iron and Steel Association, CSR China) introduce guidelines and provide CSR training programs to their members and also set standards for CSR disclosure in the industry. Model (3) explains a similar circumstance. SOEs with more training opportunities and closer relationship with the government have better CSR reporting performance compared to private firms.

On top of the driving forces from the government and associations, media attention is also an important factor that stimulates the companies' SAR performance, as shown in Model (4). However, if we integrate all four variables of main interest (POL, ASSO, SOE, and MED) into one regression model (see Model (5) in Table 10.3), political relations becomes the major factor that indicates that the central government is playing an influential role in promoting and improving the CSR reporting of Chinese enterprises.

In summary, the research shows that the central government acts like a propeller and stimulates the CSR reporting of Chinese enterprises. It is reflected by the regression results that politically related companies disclose more social information in their public reports. Analogously, due to the natural connection between SOEs and the government, listed SOEs perform better in SAR compared to private companies. Thus, ownership type becomes a key influential factor on CSR reporting. Moreover, industrial associations and CSR societies also promote good social reporting practices to their members. Companies that have more memberships in local societies have better social disclosure. Last but not least, companies with intensive media attention have much greater concern for their public image. In turn, they are more willing to improve their CSR disclosure and deliver good-quality reports to the public.

## Interview

Semi-structured face-to-face or phone interviews were applied during the third phase of the research. Denzin and Lincoln (2003, p. 64) point out that "there is inherent faith that the results are trustworthy and accurate" by using interviews. The semi-structured interview method is defined as "a context in which the interviewer has a series of questions that are in the general form of an interview schedule but is able to vary the sequence of questions . . . also, the interviewer has some latitude to ask further questions in response to what are seen as significant replies" (Bryman, 2012, p. 212). This method is suitable for conducting interviews with managers with tight schedules who cannot be accessed easily (Bernard, 2000).

Interview invitations were sent to the enterprises by email. Consent was given by 71 respondents from 39 companies. However, due to a variety of unexpected situations such as changes of schedules and difficulties in logistics, 14 appointments were cancelled. Finally, 57 participants from 31 companies were interviewed (see Table 10.4). The interviewees are all management-level personnel with direct involvement in CSR reporting in their companies.

Before conducting interviews, the background knowledge of each company was obtained according to the interview guide in Table 10.5. During the interviews, a list of guiding questions was used by the interviewer. Instant changes of preset questions were made according to the interviewees' responses. Sometimes follow-up questions were asked for responses specifically relevant to the research purpose. Under certain circumstances, some preset questions had to be dropped due to time constraints or situational contexts. The interviewer allowed the participants to speak freely and managed to get the predesigned questions or themes covered at the same time.

Most of the interview contents were manually recorded due to confidentiality concerns of the participants. Only nine interviewees permitted the researcher to use a digital recorder. The interviews lasted from 30 to 40 minutes. Before analyzing and interpreting the interview contents, the data were recorded and sorted.

*Table 10.4* Sample distribution of interviews

| Industry | Number of companies [number of interviewees] | | | |
|---|---|---|---|---|
| | SOE | Private firms | Foreign-Invested companies /MNCs | Total |
| High-profile | 8[18] | 6[9] | 5[7] | 19[34] |
| Low-profile | 4[5] | 3[7] | 5[12] | 12[23] |
| Total | 12[23] | 9[16] | 10[19] | 31[57] |

*Table 10.5* Interview guide

The participants were provided with the following information by sending the interview confirmation through email before the interviews. This information was further clarified before each interview started.

1  Title of the research
2  Responsible research team members' names and contact information
3  Research purpose and outline
4  Duration of the interview
5  Ethics and confidentiality
6  Rights of interviewees
7  Documentation of the information collected from interviewees

### Interview results

The results indicate that in general the most common media to disclose CSR information are the annual report and CSR or sustainability report. Of the companies being interviewed, 74 percent maintain a CSR column on their websites. Most companies have been reporting for one to four years. Only two foreign companies indicated that they have been reporting for more than six years in China. Additionally, it was also found that only around 32 percent of the interviewed companies have their social reports checked The most common reason was to give the information credibility. For those that did not get assurance, the most common reason was that there was "no demand for external assurance" or it was a "management decision to not do it." During the interviews, each interviewee was asked to rate the factors listed in Table 10.6 by importance. Overall, it shows that "government policies" and "legal obligations and requirements" are the top two motivating factors in the decision to disclose CSR information with a rating of "quite important." "Community concerns," "parent company's instruction," "corporate image," "shareholder/investor," "employee," and "financial institution's concerns" also have significant influence on the decision with ratings of "important" and "quite important". The strong importance of the top five factors is consistent with the discussions in Chapters 3–9. The factors that most interviewees considered "slightly important" were "to satisfy society's CSR concerns," "to follow other industrial players' practice," and "to increase profit."

Table 10.6 Motivation to report social information

| Factors | Industry type [Number of companies] (Number of interviewees) | | | | Company type [Number of companies] (Number of interviewees) | | | | | | Overall | |
|---|---|---|---|---|---|---|---|---|---|---|---|---|
| | High-profile industry [19](34) | | Low-profile industry [12](23) | | SOEs [12](23) | | Private companies [9](16) | | Foreign companies [10](19) | | | |
| | Mean | Ranking | Mean | Ranking | Mean | Ranking | Mean | Ranking | Mean | Ranking | Mean | ranking |
| To follow government's CSR policies and instructions | 3.46 | 1 | 3.29 | 1 | 3.32 | 1 | 3.28 | 2 | 3.24 | 1 | 3.32 | 1 |
| To meet legal obligations and requirements | 3.34 | 2 | 3.24 | 3 | 3.19 | 4 | 3.31 | 1 | 3.22 | 2 | 3.26 | 2 |
| To satisfy customer concerns | 3.06 | 5 | 3.16 | 4 | 3.21 | 3 | 3.22 | 3 | 3.21 | 3 | 3.17 | 3 |
| To satisfy community concerns with operations | 3.29 | 3 | 3.13 | 5 | 3.15 | 5 | 3.03 | 5 | 3.18 | 5 | 3.16 | 4 |
| To follow parent/holding company's instruction | 3.12 | 4 | 3.06 | 6 | 3.23 | 2 | 2.90 | 8 | 3.21 | 3 | 3.10 | 5 |
| To improve corporate image | 3.04 | 6 | 3.26 | 2 | 2.82 | 7 | 3.22 | 4 | 3.14 | 6 | 3.09 | 6 |
| To meet shareholder/investor's information demand | 2.88 | 7 | 2.98 | 7 | 3.03 | 6 | 2.67 | 9 | 2.13 | 10 | 2.74 | 7 |
| To satisfy employee concerns | 2.32 | 8 | 2.78 | 8 | 2.57 | 8 | 3.01 | 6 | 2.56 | 8 | 2.65 | 8 |
| To satisfy financial institution concerns | 1.38 | 9 | 2.18 | 10 | 1.89 | 10 | 2.98 | 7 | 2.87 | 7 | 2.26 | 9 |
| To satisfy CSR societies' concerns | 0.84 | 13 | 1.56 | 11 | 2.12 | 9 | 1.78 | 13 | 2.56 | 8 | 1.77 | 10 |
| To follow other industrial players' practice | 0.96 | 11 | 2.56 | 9 | 1.61 | 11 | 1.86 | 12 | 0.83 | 14 | 1.56 | 11 |
| To satisfy supplier concerns | 1.08 | 10 | 1.35 | 12 | 0.98 | 13 | 2.03 | 10 | 1.68 | 11 | 1.42 | 12 |
| To increase profits | 0.77 | 14 | 0.67 | 14 | 0.86 | 14 | 2.01 | 11 | 1.46 | 12 | 1.15 | 13 |
| To adapt to industrial practice | 0.98 | 12 | 0.73 | 13 | 1.23 | 12 | 0.67 | 14 | 1.32 | 13 | 0.99 | 14 |

Note: Level of importance: 0 = unimportant; 1 = slightly important; 2 = important; 3 = quite important; 4 = highly important

As shown in Table 10.6, political and legal forces are more important for companies from high-profile industries with the highest mean values of 3.46 and 3.34, respectively. The most common reason is because the government and regulatory bodies or authorities have effective enforcement of CSR regulations or instructions for high-profile industries. According to several interviewees from the mining and heavy industries, due to the frequent media exposure of industrial accidents and pollutions, the government and industry regulatory bodies have strengthened their supervision and control on CSR aspects, especially on safety and environmental issues. Two interviewees from the food-processing industry provided a similar explanation. Compared to other high-profile industries, their focuses of social reporting were more on product quality and the safety of food ingredients.

It is interesting to find that the legal factor is one of the top three drivers for SOEs. The most common answers from the interviewees are "we are acting as a CSR model for other enterprises" and "voluntary compliance of CSR regulations is one of the most basic criteria." In comparison, private and foreign firms treat both political and legal documents as the most important considerations for CSR disclosure. Many interviewees from private companies indicated that "regional or local governments have held meetings with private entrepreneurs on a regular basis for delivering and interpreting policy (legal) documents issued by the central government (regulatory authorities)." One interviewee gave a more straightforward answer. He said "to act as a 'good student' is important for us to keep good relationship with the government. Teachers always prefer obedient students and take more care of them." For foreign companies, the most common reason is "the government has close supervision on many CSR dimensions, especially on environment, labor and product quality aspects. The enforcement placed on foreign firms is even stricter than other types of enterprises." Another major reason for conducting CSR reporting is that branches or subsidiaries in China have to follow their parent company's reporting practice and instructions to disclose CSR information.

On top of the above findings, all the interviewees expressed their keen attention on stakeholders' demand for CSR transparency. When producing CSR reports, they try to disclose as much social information of concern to the public and different stakeholder groups. Many of them also mentioned that CSR reporting can inform the government and stakeholders of the company's attitude to CSR and the ability to promote sustainability and to be a good corporate citizen. In addition, it can provide a benchmark for best practice in the industries and drive the companies' sustainable development in a positive direction.

## Conclusion

It is worth noting that the similar results of the regression model and the interviews appear to suggest that government's influence on the company's CSR reporting behavior is stronger than other factors. In addition, legal obligations and stakeholders' concerns also account for a significant weight during the CSR reporting process of enterprises in China. Overall, the findings are generally in line with the discussions in Chapters 4, 7, and 9. However, when interpreted together, a slightly different story appears and shows mixed support for different CSR theories. To generate a clearer picture, Chapter 11 will present a thorough discussion on the research findings.

# 11 Further discussion and conclusions

## A multilayered CSR reporting framework of SOEs

Based on the findings from the previous chapters, a multilayered CSR reporting framework of SOEs, which is composed of a top-down model (Figure 11.1) and a bottom-up model (Figure 11.2), is constructed.

### Top-down model

With the rapid development of global economic integration and in response to calls to increase consumer confidence in international markets, sustainable development and CSR have come into the spotlight. Businesses worldwide started disclosing information about sustainability or CSR performance in the form of annual reports. The GRI was born during this stage to guide companies producing CSR reports. For many international enterprises, social reporting is an educational process by which responsible competitiveness can be improved (Lim and Tsutsui, 2012).

Along with the progress of globalization, China is facing many shocks and challenges. China is still in its transitional period from a planned economy to a market economy, which the government calls a "socialist market economy with Chinese characteristics." China is following a preferred policy for economic development; that is to say, a "middle way economy," as suggested by Samuelson in 2008.[1] Under the "middle way economy" theory, not too much freedom is given to market forces and definitely also not too little. At this stage, economic and social organs are not entirely ready to adjust themselves for new global CSR climate changes. To facilitate this development, the state has to establish regulations and laws, and introduce appropriate competition policies during the transition process (IMF, 2000).

During the past two decades, China's development has attracted worldwide attention. In order to ensure its continuous economic growth and to gain for itself a good position in the competitive global market, China has to improve its domestic business environment and image in order to attract additional foreign partners and investors. Especially after 2008, the impact of the international

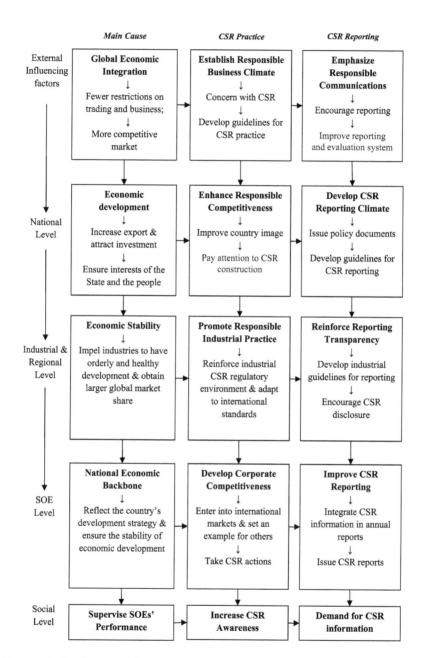

|  | *Main Cause* | *CSR Practice* | *CSR Reporting* |
|---|---|---|---|
| External Influencing factors | **Global Economic Integration** ↓ Fewer restrictions on trading and business; ↓ More competitive market | **Establish Responsible Business Climate** ↓ Concern with CSR ↓ Develop guidelines for CSR practice | **Emphasize Responsible Communications** ↓ Encourage reporting ↓ Improve reporting and evaluation system |
| National Level | **Economic development** ↓ Increase export & attract investment ↓ Ensure interests of the State and the people | **Enhance Responsible Competitiveness** ↓ Improve country image ↓ Pay attention to CSR construction | **Develop CSR Reporting Climate** ↓ Issue policy documents ↓ Develop guidelines for CSR reporting |
| Industrial & Regional Level | **Economic Stability** ↓ Impel industries to have orderly and healthy development & obtain larger global market share | **Promote Responsible Industrial Practice** ↓ Reinforce industrial CSR regulatory environment & adapt to international standards | **Reinforce Reporting Transparency** ↓ Develop industrial guidelines for reporting ↓ Encourage CSR disclosure |
| SOE Level | **National Economic Backbone** ↓ Reflect the country's development strategy & ensure the stability of economic development | **Develop Corporate Competitiveness** ↓ Enter into international markets & set an example for others ↓ Take CSR actions | **Improve CSR Reporting** ↓ Integrate CSR information in annual reports ↓ Issue CSR reports |
| Social Level | **Supervise SOEs' Performance** | **Increase CSR Awareness** | **Demand for CSR information** |

*Figure 11.1* Top-down model

financial crisis and the anticipated effects of climate change on the world economy, the environment, and the community have made the transformation of China's economic growth an urgent necessity.

To meet these challenges, China has chosen the way of sustainable development. Not only for meeting the calls of the international community but also for the need of sustainable growth itself, the Chinese government at all levels attaches great importance to CSR and sustainable development. Figure 5.2 shows the related CSR regulations and measures issued by the relevant governmental organizations, local governments, and industrial organizations that have created a better environment. These regulations and measures have therefore directed and promoted CSR performance and pushed forward the process of sustainable development of enterprises. In 2008, Chinese President Hu Jintao made a speech during the APEC CEO summit on the subject of CSR. He pointed out that "with the background of upgraded development of economic globalization, enterprise leaders should have the view of global responsibility, actively adopt the idea of social responsibility into business strategies, follow the prevailing business practices and local legislations and use their best efforts in their pursuit of the unification of economic interest and social welfare." During the same year, great importance was attached to CSR in the 17th National Congress of the Communist Party of China, as social reporting was seen as an effective way for Chinese enterprises to communicate with their stakeholders and the outside world. Afterward, attention was paid to localize international CSR initiatives (such as GRI, Accountability, SA 8000, ISO26000) with Chinese characteristics.

In 2008, the Chinese government encouraged the growth of sustainability reporting with the issuance of SASAC's 2008 document on CSR implementation by SOEs. In the document, it is clearly stated that issuing CSR reports is one of the important CSR practices of SOEs. In response to the government's call, SOEs as the backbone of the national economy need to set an example for CSR reporting and proactively improve their reporting performance. As shown by the content analysis in Chapter 5, the overall coverage and quantity of CSR disclosure increased sharply as a result, especially in 2008. In consideration of all this evidence, it can be concluded that the social reporting practices of SOEs is strongly influenced and led by the state and the CCP. In addition to the above political and economic considerations, building CSR awareness in China is also accompanied by market and institutional factors (*see* Figure 11.1). However, the initial motive of the CSR reform in China was to ensure the interests of the state and the people. From this perspective, social reporting of SOEs is more related to political and economic issues.

### Bottom-up model

CSR reporting has attracted considerable public attention. The mass media play a role of supervision and consumers have become an important driving force in compelling enterprises to fulfill their social responsibilities and dis-close more CSR information in their reports. When scandals occur or when unethical behaviors are being revealed, especially by the media and con-sumer groups, the enterprises involved react quickly to improve their CSR reporting practices by being self-critical in an effort to restore their repu-tation and business image. Additionally, many other enterprises voluntar-ily disclose more social information in order to distinguish themselves from those "offending" companies. On the other hand, industrial accidents and scandals stimulate the industrial regulatory bodies and the government to promote and standardize social reporting practices in China. As mentioned in Chapter 4, the government and its authorities have issued many important policy documents and initiatives to guide Chinese enterprises in conducting social reporting activities in the fourth quarter of 2008, immediately after the occurrence of several serious industrial accidents and scandals. Through this, the government aims to build a sustainable business environment, restore consumer's confidence and improve the image of the state in the interna-tional community.

To simplify the top-down and bottom-up models and to combine them into a cohesive whole, Figure 11.3 provides an overview of the factors involved. It provides insights into the various factors that have stimulated the devel-opment of social reporting of SOEs in China. In contrast to *Accountability*'s framework, in this study the demand for business expansion is not found as an endogenous driver of social reporting development. A press release by Kinross and Render[2] in November 2009 about the top 10 values of organizations in the international market showed that social responsibility was fourth in 2006 and seventh in 2009 (Holme, 2010). This points to a lowering of the impor-tance of CSR at a time of recession. However, in China, a contrasting result is identified in the current research, where increasing trends from different perspectives are found in the SOEs' social reporting practices, especially dur-ing the recession period from 2008 to 2010. Thus, market need is clearly not a major factor that drives the SOEs' social reporting practices. This further supports the beliefs that "the central government is pushing SOEs to publish CSR reports as a way to improve the brand, reputation and competitiveness of Chinese companies" (KPMG, 2011, p. 24) and that the image of the state is improved at the same time (see *the bottom of* Figure 11.2). Therefore, these findings demonstrate that the CSR reporting practice of SOEs in China is unique, and the origin is from the special nature of the Chinese political and economic system. Theoretically, as Deegan, (2006) demonstrates, CSR theo-ries (LT, ST, etc.) should not be treated as distinct theories because "they have been developed from a similar philosophical background and provide comple-mentary and overlapping perspectives" (Islam and Deegan, 2008, p. 853). In this study, it is observed that PET is powerful in explaining the social reporting situation of SOEs in China, while LT and ST are also prevalent but of much lesser significance.

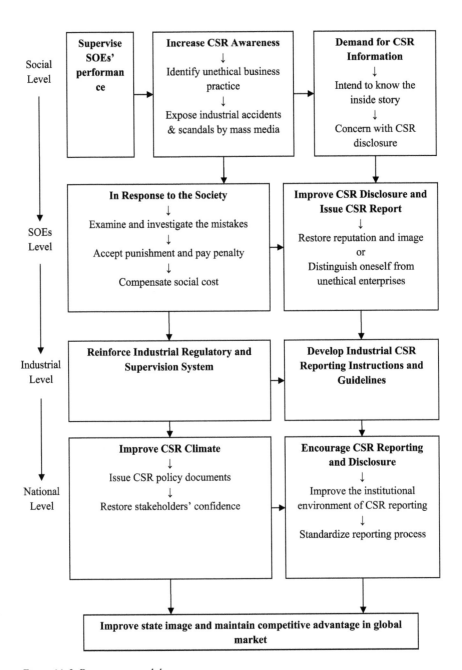

*Figure 11.2* Bottom-up model

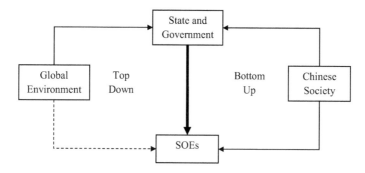

*Figure 11.3* CSR reporting drivers of SOEs in China

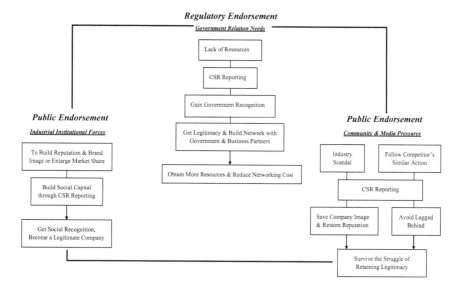

*Figure 11.4* CSR reporting framework of private firms and MNCs

## CSR reporting framework of private and multinational enterprises

The findings of Chapters 7 and 9 indicate that private and multinational enterprises deliver similar behaviors in social reporting. Higher quality information is only disclosed in some aspects, such as environment, labor, and product quality. Most likely, they only select key stakeholders to report their CSR issues. As shown in Figure 11.4, their social reporting practice is mainly stimulated by the forces from three aspects: (1) government relation needs, (2) industrial institutional forces, and (3) community and media pressures. These three aspects can be classified into two types of legitimacy, regulatory endorsement and public endorsement. According to Deephouse (1996, p. 1029), "regulatory endorsement means the acceptance of an organization by the state agencies that formally regulate it; public endorsement means the acceptance of an organization by the general public."

### Government relation needs

Studies on China indicate that private firms and foreign-invested companies suffer from high transaction costs due to the government's policies on resource allocation (Nee, 1992; Tsang, 1996). Therefore, regulatory endorsement could directly affect a company's profitability and long-term survival. The content analysis results show that private enterprises and foreign-invested companies have high involvement in CSR activities, which is in line with the government's concerns, such as employment of laid-off workers, donations, environmental protection (although some private enterprises and foreign companies have pollution scandals), community support, and quality control of products. These companies intend to raise the government's awareness of their existence and importance through performing and disclosing government-oriented CSR activities. In Chapters 4 and 5, it is mentioned that SOEs are superior to other types of enterprises in obtaining various resources from the government. Therefore, in order to strive for the government's recognition, gain more resources, and reduce networking costs, private and multinational companies keep improving CSR disclosure in the aforementioned aspects. Their final purpose is to get legitimacy in the government's mind.

Besides, based on the data collected for the empirical study in Chapter 10, it is noted that a number of private enterprises have political relationships. Among the observed private firms, about 18 percent of the entrepreneurs have membership in the NPC, and 36 percent of them are members of the CPPCC. These political relations might help to build connections with government officials and business partners in China. As suggested by Mintzberg (1983, p. 45), "organizations should always give special consideration to government officials because they represent the ultimate legislative authority of society and establish the rules within which every organization must function."

### Industrial and institutional forces

As discussed in the previous chapters, in response to the "walking out" policy, more and more private companies have started to expand their businesses in overseas markets. As for foreign-invested enterprises (MNCs), due to lower labor and operating costs, many of them have chosen China as their manufacturing powerhouse. Some other foreign companies, such as firms from the retailing, food and beverage, and electronic devices industries, have looked at China as an emerging market due to the rise in the purchasing power of Chinese consumers.

Therefore, both private and foreign-invested enterprises are actively seeking social capital from overseas or domestic communities through communicating CSR information with important stakeholders to enhance their corporate reputations and brand image—and in turn to build up competitive advantage and obtain considerable market share. According to the content analysis in Chapter 6, private companies disclose a large quantity of information related to product quality and community involvement in their social reports and websites, indicating their eagerness to create a brand image in the overseas markets. As for foreign-invested companies, in order to meet "institutionally prescribed expectations," companies may choose to change their organizational structures (DiMaggio and Powell, 1983). For instance, more than 70 Wal-Mart stores in China have established labor unions due to the increasing concern with labor issues by the community.[3]

### Community and media informational pressures

Based on the results reported in the previous chapters, it is noted that increasing freedom and transparency in the mass media in China has become an important driving force for companies to conduct CSR activities or to make responses to their industrial scandals and incidents through social reporting. Furthermore, pressures also come from the sharp competition in the market. For example, many private firms and foreign companies voluntarily disclose CSR information because their competitors have taken similar actions. In the final analysis, the ultimate source of this pressure most likely comes from communities and consumers, as these companies have strong intentions to maintain their good reputation and competitive position in the market and do not want to lag behind others in the marketplace.

As pointed out by Ahlstrom and Bruton (2001, p. 80), "firms are legitimized by their environments if they survive and prosper, and firms can also proactively build legitimacy to enhance their long-term growth prospects, which is especially vital for firms based on transition economies with a weak institutional environment." Therefore, the need for social reporting leads enterprises in China to collect information on their CSR activities. Through this manner, it helps to create a benchmark and make improvements on the CSR practices of private enterprises and foreign-invested companies in China and to achieve long-term development.

### Conclusions

Prior studies have discussed widely the approaches of and incentives for social reporting in Western economies. In recent years, although there has been considerable interest in research applied to the developing world, there is still significant scope to address CSR research in these countries. This study, therefore, fills an important gap and identifies the major drivers of the development of social reporting practices in China, the largest developing country and the second-largest economy in the world. A multilayered framework that reflects the uniqueness of the Chinese situation has been constructed to explain the development and drivers of social reporting in China. The results of this study demonstrate that the Chinese government acts as an engine leading and driving the social reporting practices of SOEs. In response to the policy documents released by the CCP and various government authorities, or in order to obtain the government's recognition and to strive for more resources, SOEs, private enterprises, and foreign-invested companies (MNCs) have made substantial improvements in social reporting. However, this is only in terms of the reporting quantity and coverage. It appears that insufficient effort is being placed on the quality of disclosure. It is also noted that the central government has economic, political, and social incentives to promote, encourage, and control the development of social reporting. Furthermore, many enterprises in China appear to use social reporting as a window-dressing instrument for improving or enhancing brand image and reputation rather than for long-term corporate development.

This study contributes to the extant literature and is the first in Western academia to report, from an indigenous perspective, the integrated results of content analysis, empirical research, and interview analysis of social reporting by three types of Chinese enterprises and to develop a unique multilayered framework to present the evolution of social reporting in this country. Theoretically, the application of PET and LT to explain CSR reporting has been widely discussed and explored in countries with well-developed capitalist systems. This is probably the first research to add such insight to PET and LT for explaining the social reporting practice of the largest socialist and transitional economy in the world. In addition, the use of GRI as an evaluation tool of reporting quantity and quality provides opportunities for scholars to conduct comparative studies in the future. Finally, it is hoped that this study can provide a point of reference for Chinese enterprises to improve their social reporting quality and provide guidance for stakeholders to evaluate social reports objectively.

There are limitations to this research that should be borne in mind. The research has concentrated on a limited number of the largest enterprises, so any inferences about all Chinese companies generally should be made with care. Finally, future researches may undertake cross-country analyses of the developing world to investigate and compare the evolution patterns and key drivers of social reporting development.

## Notes

1 On December 6, 2008, Samuelson was unable to attend the first Global Management Forum held in Shanghai due to health problems. Pedro Nueno read out the letter Samuelson prepared for the Forum. People often treat this letter as his "testament" on China.
2 Kinross and Render is an international full-service public relations consultancy in London. They provide expertise in CSR, crisis relations, international campaign management, and so on. They conducted a global survey about CSR issues in 2009 and based on the survey result, they issued a press released entitled, "Companies declare allegiance to their people."
3 News from World Labour dated March 5, 2015, available at www.worldlabour.org/chi/node/714.

# References

AA & WTO. (2009), *Responsible competitiveness in China 2009-seizing the low carbon opportunity for green development, Accountability and WTO tribune*, available at www.csr-china. net/ind/nationalcsr/files/%E5%9B%BD%E5%AE%B6%E8%B4%A3%E4%BB%BB %E7%AB%9E%E4%BA%89%E5%8A%9B%EF%BC%882009%EF%BC%89%E7 %A0%94%E7%A9%B6%E6%8A%A5%E5%91%8A%EF%BC%88%E8%8B%B1- %E6%96%87%E7%89%88%EF%BC%89.pdf

Adams, C. A., and Harte, G. (1999), *Towards corporate accountability for equal opportunities performance, ACCA Occasional Research Paper No. 26*, London, Certified Accountants Education Trust.

Adams, C. A., Hill, W. Y., and Roberts, C. B. (1995), *Environmental, employee and ethical reporting in Europe*, London, Certified Accountants Educational Trust.

Advice. (2002), *Advices on deepening the reform of internal personal, labor and distribution systems, issued by state-owned assets supervision and administration commission of the state council*, available at www.sasac.gov.cn/n1180/n20240/n7291323/11898746.html (assessed July 13, 2014)

Aerts, W., and Cormier, D. (2009), 'Media legitimacy and corporate environmental communication', *Accounting, Organizations and Society*, 34(1): 1–27.

Ahlstrom, D., and Bruton, G. D. (2001), 'Learning from successful local private firms in China: establishing legitimacy', *The Academy of Management Executive*, 15(4): 72–83.

Alcañiz, E., Herrera, A., Pérez, R., and Alcami, J. (2010), 'Latest evolution of academic research in corporate social responsibility: an empirical analysis', *Social Responsibility Journal*, 6(3): 332–344.

Al-Tuwaijri, S. A., Christensen, T. E., and Hughes, K. E. (2004), 'The relations among environmental disclosures, environmental performance, and economic performance: a simultaneous equations approach', *Accounting, Organizations and Society*, 29(5–6): 447–471.

Amaeshi, K. M., Adi, B. C., Ogbechie, C., and Olufemi, O. A. (2006), 'Corporate social responsibility in Nigeria: Western mimicry or indigenous influences?', *Journal of Corporate Citizenship*, 24(winter): 83–99.

Amran, A., and Devi, S. (2008), 'The impact of government and foreign affiliate influence on corporate social reporting, the case of Malaysia', *Managerial Auditing Journal*, 23(4): 386–404.

An, Q., Wei, L., Tang, R. T., and Song, J. Q. (2010), 'How to standardize the evaluation of environmental performance and information disclosure of listed companies', *Environmental Economy*, 5: 48–53.

Babbie, E. (2010), *The practice of social research (12th edition)*, London, Cengage Learning.

Bakija, J., and Heim, B. (2011), *How does charitable giving respond to incentives and income? New estimates from panel data*, Cambridge, MA, National Bureau of Economic Research.

Bansal, P. (2005), 'Evolving sustainability: a longitudinal study of corporate sustainable development', *Strategic Management Journal*, 26(3): 197–218.

Bansal, P., and Clelland, I. (2004), 'Talking trash: legitimacy, impression management and unsystematic risk in the context of the natural environment', *Academy of Management Journal*, 47(1): 93–103.

Barkemeyer, R., Preuss, L., and Lee, L. (2015), 'On the effectiveness of private transnational governance regimes-evaluating corporate sustainability reporting according to Global Reporting Initiative', *Journal of World Business*, 50(2): 312–325.

Barnett, M. (2007), 'Stakeholder influence capacity and the variability of financial returns to corporate social responsibility', *Academy of Management Review*, 32(3): 794–816.

Bauer, R., and Fenn, D. (1973), 'What is a corporate social audit?', *Harvard Business Review*, (January–February): 37–48.

Beams, F. A., and Fertig, P. E. (1971), 'Pollution control through social costs conversion', *Journal of Accountancy*, 1(41): 37–42.

Beaudeux, P., and Favard, E. (1975), 'L'Examen Social: Les Grandes Entreprises', *Expansion* (April): 76-85

Bebbington, J., Gray, R., and Owen, D. (1999), 'Seeing the wood for the trees: taking the pulse of social and environmental accounting', *Accounting, Auditing and Accountability Journal*, 12(1): 47–51.

Belal, A. (2001), 'A study of corporate social disclosure in Bangladesh', *Managerial Auditing Journal*, 16(5): 274–289.

Belal, A., and Momin, M. (2009), 'Corporate Social Reporting (CSR) in emerging economies: a review and future direction', *Research in Accounting in emerging economies: Emerald*, 9: 119–143.

Belal, A. R. (2002), 'Stakeholder accountability or stakeholder management: a review of UK firms' social and ethical accounting, auditing and reporting (SEAAR)', *Corporate Social Responsibility and Environmental Management*, 9(1): 8–25.

Belal, A. R. (2008), *Corporate social responsibility reporting in developing countries: the case of Bangladesh-(corporate social responsibility series)*, Farnham, UK, Ashgate Publishing Limited.

Belkaoui, A., and Karpik, P. G. (1989), 'Determinants of the corporate decision to disclose social information', *Accounting, Auditing and Accountability Journal*, 2(1): 36–51.

Berg, B. L. (2008), *Qualitative research methods for the social sciences: international edition*, Bruce L. Berg/Boston, MA, Pearson Education.

Bernard, H. R. (2000), *Social research methods: Qualitative and quantitative approaches*, Thousand Oaks, CA, Sage Publications.

Bewley, K., and Li, Y. (2000), 'Disclosure of environmental information by Canadian manufacturing companies: a voluntary disclosure perspective', *Advances in Environmental Accounting and Management*, 1: 201–226.

Bogdan, R. C., and Biklen, S. K. (2006), *Qualitative research in education: an introduction to theory and methods*, Boston, MA, Allyn & Bacon.

Bowen, F. E. (2000), 'Environmental visibility: a trigger of green organizational response?', *Business Strategy and the Environment*, 9(2): 92–107.

Brammer, S., and Pavelin, S. (2004), 'Building a good reputation', *European Management Journal*, 22(6): 704–713.

Brammer, S., and Pavelin, S. (2008), 'Factors influencing the quality of corporate environmental disclosure', *Business Strategy and the Environment*, 17(2): 120–136.

Branco, M. C., and Rodrigues, L. L. (2008), 'Corporate social responsibility and resource based perspectives', *Journal of Business Ethics*, 69(2): 111–132.

Bryman, A. (2012), *Social research methods (4th edition)*, Oxford, Oxford University Press.

Burritt, R. L., and Schaltegger, S. (2010), 'Sustainability accounting and reporting: fad or trend?', *Accounting, Auditing & Accountability Journal*, 23(7): 829–846.

Campbell, D. (2003), 'Intra- and intersectoral effects in environmental disclosures: evidence for legitimacy theory?', *Business Strategy and the Environment*, 12(6): 357–371.

Campbell, D., Moore, G., and Shrives, P. (2006), 'Cross-sectional effects in community disclosure', *Accounting, Auditing and Accountability Journal*, 19(1): 96–114.

Campbell, J. L. (2007), 'Why would corporations behave in socially responsible ways? An institutional theory of corporate social responsibility', *Academy of Management Review*, 32(3): 946–967.

Chen, W. H., Shang, L. X., and Feng, X. L. (1998), 'Conception of the building of CSR accounting', *Chinese Agricultural Accounting*, 8: 6–8. (In Chinese)

Chen, Y. Q., and Ma, L. L. (2005), 'Market response to the social responsibility accounting', *Accounting Research*, 11: 76–81. (In Chinese)

China Statistical Yearbook. (2016), *China Statistical Yearbook*, complied by National Bureau of Statistics of China, China Statistics Press.

Cho, C. H., and Patten, D. M. (2007), 'The role of environmental disclosures as tools of legitimacy: a research note', *Accounting, Organizations and Society*, 32(7–8): 639–647.

Choi, J. S. (1999), 'An investigation of the initial voluntary environmental disclosures made in Korean semi-annual financial reports', *Pacific Accounting Review*, 11(1): 73–102.

Choi, J., and Sami, H. (2012), 'Corporate transparency from the global perspective: A conceptual overview', *International Finance Review*, 13: 3–7.

Christiansen, H. (2011), *The size and composition of the SOE sector in OECD countries*, OECD Corporate Governance Working Papers, No. 5, OECD Publishing, Paris.

Churchman, C. W. (1971), 'On the facility, felicity, and morality of measuring social change', *Accounting Review*, 46(1): 30–35.

CIEL. (2008), *Classification of industries for listed companies requiring environmental verification*. Notice released by Ministry of Environmental Protection of the People's Republic of China.

Cormier, D., Gordon, I. M., and Magnan, M. (2004), 'Corporate environmental disclosure: contrasting management's perceptions with reality', *Journal of Business Ethics*, 49(2): 143–165.

Cormier, D., Magnan, M., and Van Velthoven, B. (2005), 'Environmental disclosure quality in large German companies: Economic incentives, public pressures or institutional conditions?', *European Accounting Review*, 14(1): 3–39.

Cowen, S., Ferreri, L., and Parker, L. (1987), 'The impact of corporate characteristics on social responsibility disclosure: A typology and frequency-based analysis', *Accounting, Organizations and Society*, 12(2): 111–122.

Cui, X. M. (2009), 'On the influencing factors for enterprise releasing social responsibility report: evidences from enterprise social responsibility reports by listed firms in 2008', *Journal of Nanjing Agricultural University (Social Sciences Edition)* 9(4): 40–46.

Cui, Z., Liang, X., and Lu, X. (2015), 'Prize or price? Corporate social responsibility commitment and sales performance in the Chinese private sector', *Management and Organization Review*, 11(1): 25–44.

Deegan, C. (2002), 'The legitimizing effect of social and environmental disclosures – a theoretical foundation', *Accounting, Auditing and Accountability Journal*, 15(3): 282–311.

Deegan, C. (2006), *Financial accounting theory*, Irwin, Sydney, McGraw-Hill.

Deegan, C., and Blomquist, C. (2001), 'Stakeholder influence on corporate reporting: an exploration of the interaction between the world wide fund for nature and the Australian minerals industry', paper presented at the *Third Asia Pacific Interdisciplinary Research in Accounting Conference*, Adelaide.

Deegan, C., and Blomquist, C. (2006), 'Stakeholder influence on corporate reporting: an exploration of the interaction between WWF-Australia and the Australian minerals industry', *Accounting, Organizations and Society*, 31(4–5): 343–372.

Deegan, C., and Gordon, B. (1996), 'A study of the environmental disclosure practices of Australian corporations', *Accounting and Business Research*, 26(3): 187–199.

Deegan, C., and Rankin, M. (1996), 'Do Australian companies report environmental news objectively? An analysis of environmental disclosures by firms prosecuted successfully by the environmental protection authority', *Accounting, Auditing and Accountability Journal*, 9(2): 50–67.

Deegan, C., Rankin, M., and Tobin, J. (2002), 'An examination of the corporate social and environmental disclosures of BHP from 1983–1997: A test of legitimacy theory', *Accounting, Auditing and Accountability Journal*, 15(3): 312–343.

Deegan, C., Rankin, M., and Voght, P. (2000), 'Firms' disclosure reactions to major social incidents: Australian evidence', *Accounting Forum*, 24(1): 101–130.

Deegan, C., and Soltys, S. (2007), 'Social accounting research: An Australasian perspective', *Accounting Forum*, 31: 73–89.

Deegan, C., and Unerman, J. (2006), *Financial accounting theory*, Maidenhead, UK, McGraw-Hill.

Deephouse, D. L. (1996), 'Does isomorphism legitimate?', *Academy of Management Journal*, 39(4): 1024–1039.

Deng, Q. W., and Chen, J. G. (2009), 'Implementation of social responsibility information disclosure: a case study of Wu Steel', *Finance and Accounting*, 5: 35.

Denzin, N. K. (1978), *The research act: a theoretical introduction to sociological methods*, New York, Praeger.

Denzin, N. K., and Lincoln, Y. S. (2003), *Collecting and interpreting qualitative materials (2nd edition)*, Thousand Oaks, CA, Sage Publications.

De Oliveira, J.A.P. (2006), 'Corporate citizenship in Latin America: new challenges to business', *Journal of Corporate Citizenship*, 21(spring): 17–20.

Di, C. (2015), 'From Northern Talk to Theme Report for "The Third Plenary Session" – Deng Xiao Ping and the gestation of China's reform and opening up decision', *Historiography Research in Anhui*, 1: 101–107.

Diamond, P. (2006), 'Optimal tax treatment of private contributions for public goods with and without warm glow preferences', *Journal of Public Economics*, 90(4–5): 897–919.

Dias-Sardinha, I., and Reijnders, L. (2001), 'Environmental performance evaluation and sustainability performance evaluation of organizations: an evolutionary framework', *Eco-Management and Auditing*, 8(2): 71–79.

Dierkes, M. (1979), 'Corporate social reporting in Germany: conceptual developments and practical experience', *Accounting, Organizations and Society*, 4(1–2): 87–107.

Dierkes, M., and Preston, L. (1977), 'Corporate social accounting reporting for the physical environment: a critical review and implementation proposal', *Accounting, Organizations and Society*, 2(1): 3–22.

DiMaggio, P. J., and Powell, W. W. (1983), 'The iron cage revisited: Institutional isomorphism and collective rationality in organizational fields', *American Sociological Review*, 48(2): 147–160.

Document. (1998), *Interim provisions on the administration of the right to use the land transferred in reforms of state-owned enterprises*, issued by Ministry of Land and Resources, available at www.mlr.gov.cn/zwgk/flfg/tdglflfg/200502/t20050204_635014.htm

Document. (2006), *Implementation of stock option incentive for state-controlled listed companies (Trail)*, available at www.sasac.gov.cn/n1180/n20240/n7291323/11898529.html

Epstein, M., Flamholtz, E., and McDonough, J. (1976), 'Corporate social accounting in the United States of America: State of the art and future prospects', *Accounting, Organizations and Society*, 1(1): 23–42.

Eugénio, T., Lourenço, I., and Morais, A. (2010), 'Recent developments in social and environmental accounting research', *Social Responsibility Journal*, 6(2): 286–305.

Fan, J. P. (2012), 'A preliminary analysis of the state-owned enterprises fulfilling corporate social responsibilities in the new period', *Economic Research Guide*, 18, 32–34.

Fan, J. P., Wong, T. J., and Zhang, T. Y. (2007), 'Politically connected CEOs, corporate governance and post IPO performance of China's newly partially privatized firms', *Journal of Financial Economics*, 84(2): 330–357.

Foster, D., and Jonker, J. (2005), 'Stakeholder relationships: The dialogue of engagement', *Corporate Governance*, 5(5): 51–57.

Foster, K. (2011), 'Association in the embrace of an authoritative state: State domination of society?', *Studies in Comparative International Development*, 35(4): 84–109.

Freeman, R. (1984), *Strategic management: a stakeholder approach*, Boston, MA, Pitman.

Fu, X. Q., and Zhu, W. L. (2010), 'A statistical analysis on social responsibility reports of listed companies', *Communication of Finance and Accounting*, 3: 40–42.

Fuchs, D. (2007), *Business power in global governance*, Boulder, Lynne Rienner Publishers.

Gao, M., He, J., and Liu, X. (2008), *Report on the development status of foreign economy-the cross-sectional analysis based on the first economic census*, China, Economic Science Press.

Gao, M., Li, J., and He, J. (2005), *Foreign direct investment statistics*, China, Economic Science Press.

Gao, S. S., Heravi, S., and Xiao, J. Z. (2005), 'Determinants of corporate social and environmental reporting in Hong Kong: A research note', *Accounting Forum*, 29(2): 233–242.

Garriga, E., and Mele, D. (2004), 'Corporate social responsibility theories: Mapping the territory', *Journal of Business Ethics*, 53(1): 51–71.

Garwin, D. A. (1983), 'Can industry self-regulation work?', *California Management Review*, 25(4): 37–52.

Ghosh, K. (2015), 'Developing organizational creativity and innovation toward a model of self-leadership, employee creativity, creativity climate and workplace innovative orientation', *Management Research Review*, 38(11): 1126–1148.

Gond, J., and Herrbach, O. (2006), 'Social reporting as an organizational learning tool? A theoretical framework', *Journal of Business Ethics*, 65(4): 359–371.

Gray, R. (2000), 'Current developments and trends in social and environmental auditing, reporting and attestation: A review and comment', *International Journal of Auditing*, 4(3): 247–268.

Gray, R. (2001), 'Thirty years of social accounting, reporting and auditing: What (if anything) have we learnt?', *Business Ethics: A European Review*, 10(1): 9–15.

Gray, R. (2002), 'The social accounting project and accounting, organizations and society: Privileging engagement, imaginings, new accountings and pragmatism over critique?', *Accounting, Organizations and Society*, 27(7): 687–708.

Gray, R., Dey, C., Owen, D., Evans, R., and Zadek, S. (1997), 'Struggling with the praxis of social accounting, stakeholders, accountability, audits and procedures', *Accounting, Auditing and Accountability Journal*, 10(3): 325–364.

Gray, R., Kouhy, R., and Lavers, S. (1995), 'Corporate social and environmental reporting: A review of the literature and a longitudinal study of UK disclosure', *Accounting Auditing & Accountability Journal*, 8(2): 44–77.

Gray, R., Owen, D., and Adams, C. (1996), *Accounting and accountability: Changes and challenges in corporate social and environmental reporting*, Harlow, Prentice-Hall Europe.

Gray, R., Owen, D., and Maunders, K. (1987), *Corporate social reporting: Accounting and accountability*, London, Prentice-Hall International.

GRI. (2006), *Sustainability reporting guidelines*, Version Three, Global Reporting Initiative, available at www.globalreporting.org/resourcelibrary/G3-Guidelines-Incl-Technical-Protocol.pdf

Guan, J. Q., and Noronha, C. (2013), 'Corporate social responsibility reporting research in the Chinese academia: A critical review', *Social Responsibility Journal*, 9(1): 33–55.

Guan, J. Q., Noronha, C., and Tayles, M. E. (2013), 'Explaining social reporting of state-owned enterprises in China: A market economy with socialist characteristics', Conference presentation at the *Seventh Asia Pacific Interdisciplinary Research in Accounting*, Kobe, Japan, 25–28 July.

Guideline. (2006), *Guidelines to the state-owned enterprises directly under the central government on fulfilling corporate social responsibilities*, available at http://en.sasac.gov.cn/n1408035/c1477196/content.html

Gunawan, J. (2010), 'Perception of important information in corporate social disclosures: evidence from Indonesia', *Social Responsibility Journal*, 6(1): 62–71.

Guthrie, J., and Mathews, M. (1985), 'Corporate social accounting in Australasia, in Preston, L.E. (Ed.)', *Research in Corporate Social Performance and Policy*, 7: 251–277.

Guthrie, J., and Parker, L. (1990), 'Corporate social disclosure practice: A comparative international practice', *Advances in Public Interest Accounting*, 3: 159–175.

Hackston, D., and Milne, M. J. (1996), 'Some determinants of social and environmental disclosures in New Zealand companies', *Accounting, Auditing and Accountability Journal*, 9(1): 77–108.

Han, J. H., and Gan, S. D. (2013), 'A literature review on foreign research of corporate social responsibility accounting theory', *East China Economic Management*, 27(6): 150–154.

Han, Q. L., and Ji, Y. Y. (2010), 'The research of the relationship between corporate governance structure and social responsibility information disclosure: A case study of the food and beverage industry', *Business Culture*, 4: 57–58.

Han, Y., and Du, B. H. (2002), 'A research on CSR information disclosure issues', *Auditing: Theory and Practice*, 6: 51.

Haniffa, R. M., and Cooke, T. E. (2005), 'The impact of culture and governance on corporate social reporting', *Journal of Accounting and Public Policy*, 24(5): 391–430.

He, L. M., and Hou, T. (2009), 'A research on the disclosure of environmental performance information of power enterprises: A comparison between social responsibility reporting in China and that in foreign countries', *Communication of Finance and Accounting*, 12: 129–131.

Heilman, S. (1976), *Synagogue life: a study in symbolic interaction*, Englewood Cliffs, NJ, Prentice Hall.

Henriques, I., and Sadorsky, P. (1996), 'The role of information in coordinating environmental issues', *Academy of Management Best Paper Proceedings* (Cincinnati, OH): 1–30.

Hillman, A. J., Keim, G. D., and Schuler, D. (2004), 'Corporate political activity: A review and research agenda', *Journal of Management*, 30(6): 837–857.

Hirschland, M. J. (2006), *Corporate social responsibility and the shaping of global public policy*, New York, Palgrave Macmillan.

Ho, L. J., and Taylor, M. E. (2007), 'An empirical analysis of triple bottom-line reporting and its determinates: Evidence from the United States and Japan', *Journal of international Financial Management and Accounting*, 18(2): 123–150.

Holme, C. (2010), 'Corporate social responsibility: A strategic issue or a wasteful distraction?', *Industrial and Commercial Training*, 42(4): 179–185.

Holsti, O. R. (1969), *Content analysis for the social sciences and humanities*, Reading, MA, Addison-Wesley.

Hu, J., Dong, D., and Jin, W. (2013), 'A study on relationship between corporate social responsibility disclosure and stock market prices: Evidence from private enterprises listed in SSE', *Journal of Business Economics*, 258(4): 73–80.

Huang, Q. H., Peng, H. G., Zhong, H. W., and Zhang, E. (2009), 'Evaluating the level of responsibility management and CSR information disclosure of top 100 companies in China', *China Industrial Economics*, 10: 23–35.

Hubbard, G. (2009), 'Unsustainable reporting', in CR Debates, The Royal Institution of Great Britain (Corpo-rateRegister.com, London).

IMF. (2000), *Transition economies: an IMF perspective on progress and prospects*, IMF..

Islam, M. A., and Deegan, C. (2008), 'Motivations for an organisation within a developing country to report social responsibility information: Evidence from Bangladesh', *Accounting, Auditing & Accountability Journal*, 21(6): 850–874.

Ji, Z. (2011), 'Discussion on the development of private enterprises in China', *China Business and Trade*, 25: 247–248.

Jiang, W., Yang, D., and Zhou, C. (2006), 'The CSR appraisal system for Chinese private companies', *Statistical Research*, 7: 32–36. (In Chinese)

Jin, Z., and Zhu, Z. Q. (2010), 'Analysis of corporate social responsibility information disclosures in listed transport sector companies in China', *Railway Transport and Economy*, 5: 7–11. (In Chinese)

Jo, H., and Kim, Y. (2008), 'Ethics and disclosure: A study of the financial performance of firms in the seasoned equity offerings market', *Journal of Business Ethics*, 80(4): 855–878.

Johnson, R. D., and Greening, D. W. (1999), 'The effects of corporate governance and institutional ownership types on corporate social performance', *Academy of Management Journal*, 42(5): 564–576.

Jones, M. J. (2010), 'Accounting for the environment: Towards a theoretical perspective for environmental accounting and reporting', *Accounting Forum*, 34(2): 123–138.

Joseph, E. (2002), 'Promoting corporate social responsibility: Is market-based regulation sufficient', *New Economy*, 9(2): 96–101.

Khan, M. H. (2010), 'The effect of corporate governance elements on corporate social responsibility (CSR) reporting', *International Journal of Law and Management*, 52(2): 82–109.

KPMG. (2011), *2011 KPMG China corporate social responsibility report*, available at www.caringcompany.org.hk/doc/Sustainability_Report/R0039_en.pdf

Krippendorff, K. (1980), *Content analysis: An introduction to its methodology*. London, Sage Publications.

Kuo, L., Yeh, C. C., and Yu, H. C. (2011), 'Disclosure of corporate social responsibility and environmental management: Evidence from China', *Corporate Social Responsibility and Environmental Management*, 19(5): 273–287.

Lam, W. (2005), *China's 11th five-year plan: A roadmap for China's 'Harmonious Society?'*, Association for Asian Research Articles, available at www.asianresearch.org/articles/2756.html

Lewis, L., and Unerman, J. (1999), 'Ethical relativism: A reason for differences in corporate social reporting?', *Critical Perspectives on Accounting*, 10(4): 521–547.

Li, H. B., Meng, L. S., and Zhang, J. S. (2006), 'Why do entrepreneurs enter politics? Evidence from China', *Economic Inquiry*, 44(3): 559–578.

Li, J. M. (2004), 'On information disclosure of social responsibility accounting of enterprises', *Journal of Wuhan University of Science and Technology (Social Science Edition)*, 6(3): 8–13. (In Chinese)

Li, J. M. (2014), 'On the value of private enterprise social responsibility strategic investment under the reputation effect', 36: 180–181. (In Chinese)

Li, L. (2015), 'Response analysis of mass incidents in private enterprise labor disputes', *Journal of Xinyang Normal University*, 35(2): 40–44. (In Chinese)

Li, W. J. (2010), 'An analysis on the problems of social responsibility accounting information disclosure of listed companies in China', *Oriental Enterprise Culture*, 3: 50–52. (In Chinese)

Li, X. E., and Mu, H. L. (2010), 'The relationship between corporate social responsibility and enterprise performance: An empirical study', *Enterprise Economy*, 4: 104–107.

Li, X. E., and Peng, H. G. (2010), 'Case study of the relationship between CSR information disclosure and enterprise's reputation', *Reform of Economic System*, 3: 74–76.

Li, Y., and Zhan, Z. (2012), 'The social responsibility of private enterprises in the public crisis: Content structure and fostering mechanisms', *Social Sciences in Nanjing*, 4: 20–25. (In Chinese)

Li, Y. H., and Liu, Y. P. (2010), *Blue book of corporate social responsibility construction in China*, People Press. (In Chinese)

Li, Y. Q., and Jiang, X. (1998), 'Corporate social responsibility and information disclosure', *Forestry Finance and Accounting*, 10: 3–4. (In Chinese)

Lim, A., and Tsutsui, K. (2012), 'Globalization and commitment in corporate social responsibility: Cross-national analyses of institutional and political-economy effects', *American Sociological Review*, 77(1): 69–98.

Lin, L. W. (2010), 'Corporate social responsibility in China: Window dressing or structural change?', *Berkeley, Journal of International Law*, 28(1): 64–100.

Lin, N. (2011), 'Capitalism in China: A centrally managed capitalism (CMC) and its future', *Management and Organization Review*, 7(1): 63–96.

Lin, Y. Q., and Zhao, S. M. (2013), 'Political network strategy, system support and strategic flexibility- regulatory effect of cut-throat competition', *Management World*, 4: 82–90. (In Chinese)

Liu, X., Garcia, P., and Vredenburg, H. (2014), 'CSR adoption strategies of Chinese state oil companies: Effects of global competition and cooperation', *Social Responsibility Journal*, 10(1): 38–52.

Liu, Q., Tian, G., and Wang, X. (2011), 'The effect of ownership structure on leverage decision: New evidence from Chinese listed firms', *Journal of the Asia Pacific Economy*, 16(2): 254–276.

Liu, Y. L. (2003), 'On the improvement of accounting responsibility and financial reporting of natural monopolist enterprises: A case study of power enterprises', *Accounting Research*, 8: 17–30. (In Chinese)

Lu, D. (2002), *Economic and legal analysis of corporate social responsibility*, China, Law Press.

Lu, X., and Li, J. M. (2010), 'A research on the environmental information disclosure of Chinese listed companies: A case study of the listed manufacturing industry of A-shares firms during the period 2007–2008 in the Shanghai stock market', *Journal of Audit and Economics*, 25(3): 62–69. (In Chinese)

Luo, J. M., and Guan, Z. (2003), 'Discussion on CSR disclosure', *Economists*, 7: 152. (In Chinese)

Mackey, A., Mackey, T., and Barney, J. (2007), 'Corporate social responsibility and firm performance: Investor preference and corporate strategies', *Academy of Management Journal*, 32(3): 817–835.

Magness, V. (2006), 'Strategic posture, financial performance and environmental 29 disclosure: An empirical test of legitimacy theory', *Accounting, Auditing & Accountability Journal*, 19(4): 540–563.

Marx, K. (1990) [1867]. *Capital, volume I*. Trans. B. Fowkes, London, Penguin Books.

Mathews, M. R. (1993), *Socially responsible accounting*, London, Chapman and Hall.

Mathews, M. R. (1997), 'Twenty-five years of social and environmental accounting research: Is there a silver jubilee to celebrate?', *Accounting Auditing and Accountability Journal*, 10(2): 481alti.

MCSRR. (2011), *2011 multinationals' CSR problem report, China international council for the promotion of multinational corporation*, available at www.cicpmc.org/en/index.asp

McWilliams, A., and Siegel, D. (2000), 'Corporate social responsibility and financial performance: Correlation or misspecification?', *Strategic Management Journal*, 21(5): 603–609.

Merton, R. K. (1968), *Social theory and social structure*, New York, Free Press.

Mintzberg, H. (1983), *Power in and around organizations*, Englewood Cliffs, NJ, Prentice-Hall.

Mirfazli, E. (2008), 'Corporate social responsibility (CSR) information disclosure by annual reports of public companies listed at Indonesia Stock Exchange (IDX)', *International Journal of Islamic and Middle Eastern Finance and Management*, 1(4): 275–284.

Mobley, S. C. (1970), 'The challenges of socio-economic accounting', *The Accounting Review*, 45(4): 762–768.

Moneva, J. M., and Llena, F. (2000), 'Environmental disclosures in the annual reports of large companies in Spain', *European Accounting Review*, 9(1): 7–29.

Moon, J., and Vogel, D. (2008), 'Corporate social responsibility, government and civil society', in Crane, A., McWilliams, A., Matten, D., Moon, J. and Siegel, D. (eds.) *The Oxford handbook of corporate social responsibility*, Oxford, Oxford University Press.

Mousa, G. A. (2010), 'Stakeholder theory as an arch to manage successful legitimacy strategies', *International Journal of Critical Accounting*, 2(4): 399–418.

Nee, V. (1992), 'Organizational dynamics of market transition: hybrid forms, property rights and mixed economy in China', *Administrative Science Quarterly*, 37(1), 1–27.

Neumann, W. (2003), *Social research methods: qualitative and quantitative approaches*, Boston, MA, Allyn & Bacon.

Newson, M., and Deegan, C. (2002), 'Global expectations and their associations with corporate social disclosure practice in Australia, Singapore and South Korea', *The International Journal of Accounting*, 37: 183–213.

Noronha, C., and Kong, K.W.P. (2015), 'Corporate social disclosure: the case of China's milk product industry', in Noronha, C. (ed.) *Corporate social disclosure: critical perspectives in China and Japan*, Basingstoke: Palgrave Macmillan.

Noronha, C., Si Tou, M., and Guan, J. (2013), 'Corporate social responsibility reporting in China: an overview and comparison with major trends', *Corporate Social Responsibility and Environmental Management*, 20(1): 29–42.

Noronha, C., and Wang, S. X. (2015), 'Corporate social disclosure and performance gap: "Greenwashing" Foxconn's Shenzhen factories', in Noronha, C. (ed.) *Corporate social disclosure: critical perspectives in China and Japan*. Basingstoke: Palgrave Macmillan.

O'Dwyer, B. (2006), 'Theoretical and practical contributions of social accounting to corporate social responsibility', in Allouche, J. (ed.) *Corporate social responsibility volume 1: concepts, accountability and reporting*, New York, Palgrave Macmillan.

Orlitzky, M. (2001), 'Does firm size confound the relationship between corporate social performance and firm financial performance?', *Journal of Business Ethics*, 33(2): 167–180.

Owen, D. L. (2008), 'Chronicles of wasted time? A personal reflection on the current state of, and future prospects for, social and environmental accounting research', *Accounting, Auditing and Accountability Journal*, 21(2): 240–267.

Owen, D. L., Swift, T. A., Humphrey, C., and Bowerman, M. (2000), 'The new social audits: accountability, managerial capture or the agenda of social champions?', *European Accounting Review*, 9(1): 81–90.

Parker, L. (2005), 'Social and environmental accountability research: a view from the commentary box', *Accounting, Auditing and Accountability Journal*, 18(6): 842–860.

Patten, D. M. (1992), 'Intra-industry environmental disclosures in response to the Alaskan oil spill: a note on legitimacy theory', *Accounting, Organizations and Society*, 17(5): 471–475.

Perrini, F. (2006), 'The practitioner's perspective on non-financial reporting', *California Management Review*, 48(2): 73–103.

Porter, M. E., and Kramer, M. R. (2006), 'Strategy and society: the link between competitive advantage and corporate social responsibility', *Harvard Business Review*, 84(12): 78–92.

Porter, M. E., and Van der Linde, C. (1995), 'Toward a new conception of the environment-competitiveness relationship', *Journal of Economic Perspectives*, 9(4): 97–118.

Preston, L. (1981), 'Research on corporate social reporting: directions for development', *Accounting, Organizations and Society*, 6(3): 255–262.

Qiao, M. Z., and Liu, F. C. (2010), 'A study of Chinese state-owned enterprises' CSR on perspective of nature and function', *East China Economic Management*, 24(3): 86–90. (In Chinese)

Rahman, N., Zain, M., and Al-Haj, N. (2011), 'CSR disclosures and its determinants: evidence from Malaysian government link companies', *Social Responsibility Journal*, 7(2): 181–201.

Raman, S. R. (2006), 'Corporate social reporting in India: A view from the top', *Global Business Review*, 7(2): 313–324.

Randolph, W. (1995), 'Dynamic income, progressive taxes, and the timing of charitable contributions', *Journal of Political Economy*, 103(4): 709–738.

Rasche, A., and Kell, G. (Eds.) (2010), *The United Nations global compact: achievements, trends and challenges*, Cambridge, Cambridge University Press.

Reverte, C. (2009), 'Determinants of corporate social responsibility disclosure ratings by Spanish listed firms', *Journal of Business Ethics*, 88(2): 351–366.

Roberts, R. W. (1992), 'Determinants of corporate social responsibility disclosure: An application of stakeholder theory', *Accounting, Organizations & Society*, 17(6): 595–612.

Schmidheiny, S. (2006), 'A view of corporate citizenship in Latin America', *Journal of Corporate Citizenship*, 21(spring): 21–24.

Shan, H. L. (2000), 'A discussion on corporate accounting information disclosure', *Northern Economy and Trade*, 2: 106–107. (In Chinese)

Shi, G. Y. (2001), 'China's foreign economic trade in the 21st century', in Brahm, L. J. (ed.) *China's century: the awakening of the next economic powerhouse*, Singapore and New York, John Wiley and Sons, 119–125.

Shi, G. Y., and Wang, H. (2010), 'Market value management of A-share market in China-2009 annual report (4): Corporate governance, information disclosure and investor relations management', *Capital Markets*, 5: 44–49. (In Chinese)

Shin, K. Y. (2014), *Corporate social responsibility reporting in China*, Berlin, Springer.

Simon, F. L. (1992), 'Marketing green products in the triad', *Columbia Journal of World Business*, 27(3/4): 268–285.

Si Tou, C.M.I., and Noronha, C. (2015), 'The trend of corporate social disclosure in mainland Chinese listed companies: A longitudinal observation', in Noronha, C. (ed.) *Corporate social disclosure: critical perspectives in China and Japan*, Basingstoke, Palgrave Macmillan.

Sun, W. (2010), 'Exploration and discussion on the development path of small and medium sized private enterprises', *Management and Technology of SME*, 22: 92–93. (In Chinese)

Tao, G. H. (2013), 'Some considerations on the "Two Doublings" and the social responsibility of state-owned enterprises', *China Business and Market*, 27(10): 69–73.

Tsang, E.W.K. (1996), 'In search of legitimacy: The private entrepreneur in China', *Entrepreneurship: The Theory and Practice*, 21(1): 21–30.

Ullmann, A. (1985), 'Data in search of a theory: A critical examination of the relationships among social performance, social disclosure, and economic performance of U.S. firms', *Academy of Management Review*, 10(3): 540–558.

Unerman, J. (2000), 'Methodological issues – reflections on quantification in corporate social reporting content analysis', *Accounting, Auditing & Accountability Journal*, 13(5): 667–681.

Visser, W. (2008), 'Corporate social responsibility in developing countries', in Crane, C., Matten, D., McWilliams, A. and Siegel, D. (eds.) *The Oxford handbook of corporate social responsibility*, Oxford, Oxford University Press, 473–479.

Wang, D. (2010), 'Discussion on the path carrying out its social duty for the state-owned enterprises', *Theory Monthly*, 5: 160–163. (In Chinese)

Wang, L. (2010), 'The building of social responsibility performance system in insurance companies', *South China Finance*, 1: 66–70. (In Chinese)

Wang, Y. (2015), 'Analysis of labor relations from Internet perspective', *Statistics and Management*, 10: 134–135.

Wang, Y., and Li, T. (2005), 'Research on capital operation of private enterprises', *Journal of Central University of Finance and Economics*, 7: 48–51. (In Chinese)

Webb, E. J., Campbell, D. T., Schwartz, R. D., and Sechrest, L. (1966), *Unobtrusive measures: nonreactive measures in the social sciences*, Chicago, Rand McNally.

Weber, R. P. (1990), *Basic content analysis*. Newbury Park, CA, Sage Publications.

Weidenbaum, M. L. (1999), *Business and Government in the Global Marketplace (6th edition)*, Upper Saddle River, NJ, Prentice Hall.

Wikipedia. (2011), *List of accidents and disasters by death toll*. Updated to February 2011, available at http://en.wikipedia.org/wiki/List_of_accidents_and_disasters_by_death_toll

Williams, S. (1999), 'Voluntary environmental and social accounting disclosure practices in the Asia-Pacific Region: An international empirical test of political economy theory', *The International Journal of Accounting*, 34(2): 209–238.

Wu, J. M. (2005), 'Organizational operation of industry association: An analysis from the perspective of social capital', *Management World*, 10: 83–91. (In Chinese)

Wu, Y. M. (2013), 'A survey-based discussion on perception and attitude towards CSR in China', *Creative Education*, 4(4): 267–272.

Xia, H., and Li, Y. (2010), 'A content analysis of listed companies' social responsibility reports', *Communication of Finance and Accounting*, 12: 99–102. (In Chinese)

Xu, C. C., Feng, D. B., and Ai, D. Z. (2011), 'Policy research on corporate social responsibility and reform of state-owned enterprises in old industrial base', *Northeast Asia Forum*, 20(3): 98–103.

Xu, C. C., and Zhou, J. (2011), 'CSR comparative study between state owned and private enterprises', *Economic Review*, 10: 23–26. (In Chinese)

Xu, X. (2013), *Statistical research on the development and effects of foreign economy in China*, China, China Renmin University Press.

Xu, X., Gao, M., Xu, L., and Liu, X. (2016), *A study on the development of China's foreign capital economy and its effect*, Scientific Research Institute of Statistics of the National Bureau of Statistics, available at www.stats.gov.cn/tjzs/tjsj/tjcb/dysj/201603/t20160317_1332348.html

Yang, C. F. (2009), 'Empirical study on the influential factors of social responsibility of Chinese enterprises', *Economist*, 1: 66–76. (In Chinese)

Yang, Y. (2013), 'The analysis of the current CSR status of private enterprises', *Forward Position*, 333(7): 122–124.

Yang, Y., and Chen, M. L. (2010), 'An analysis of the 2008 corporate social responsibility reports of listed companies', *Accounting Students*, 12: 94–95. (In Chinese)

Yu, M. G., and Pan, H. B. (2008), 'The relationship between politics, institutional environments and private enterprises' access to bank loans', *Management World*, 8: 9–21. (In Chinese)

Zhang, D. R. (2002), 'An exploration of enterprise voluntary information disclosure', *Finance and Accounting Monthly*, 9: 22–23. (In Chinese)

Zhang, J. J., and Zhang, Z. X. (2005), 'Political strategies of Chinese private enterprises', *Management World*, 7: 94–105. (In Chinese)

Zhang, J. R., Guo, H. T., Li, B., and Wang, W. (2009), 'The influence of financial situation on environmental information disclosure in China's Chemical Industry', *International Journal of Global Environmental Issues*, 9(3): 272–286.

Zhang, Q., and Fung, H. G. (2006), 'China's social capital and financial performance of private enterprises', *Journal of Small Business and Enterprise Development*, 13(2): 198–207.

Zhang, Z. (2004), 'On mechanisms for the reinforcement of information disclosure of joint-stock companies', *Forward Position in Economics*, 11: 186–188. (In Chinese)

Zhao, Y., Zhang, X., and Wang, Z. W. (2012), *Report on fulfillment social responsibility of central state-owned enterprises*, China, China Economic Publishing House.

Zheng, S. B. (2010), 'A research of the improvement of information disclosure on organizational performance of listed companies in China', *Consumer Guide*, 4: 66–67. (In Chinese)

Zhu, B. (2002), 'The sustainable development of private enterprises', *Enterprise Economy*, 6: 66–67. (In Chinese)

Zhu, L., Zhang, M., and Zhang Y. (2013), 'The inspiration of zero energy consumption building in developed countries', *Chinese and Foreign Entrepreneurs*, 445(12): 196–197. (In Chinese)

# Appendix 1

## Summary of 2011 scandals in China

| Company name (country) [company type] | CSR problems | Scandal happened in China |
|---|---|---|
| Carrefour (France) and Walmart (U.S.) [Foreign-invested enterprise] | Human rights: Damage public interests | Jan., 2011, Carrefour and Walmart stores in China were caught using illegal pricing methods: (1) stating a fake original price when advertising sale items; (2) attracting customers by advertising low prices; (3) offering a fake promotion; (4) using misleading prices. (*Source: www.eeo.com.cn/ens/homepage/ briefs/2011/02/10/192905.shtml; www.cicpmc. org/en/detail.asp?id=3157&Channel=2&Clas sID=14*) |
| Toyota Motor Corporation (Japan) [Foreign-invested enterprise] | Human rights: Damage public interests | Toyota recalled over 5 million vehicles in the world in 2010, but only 70,000 in China in 2011. Toyota officials only said that there had been no complaints in China about the sort of problem US drivers have reported. Toyota China even refused to make any explanation for the recall to Chinese consumers. Comments from the public pointed out "We firmly oppose Toyota's discrimination against Chinese consumers." (*Source: en.wikipedia.org/ wiki/2009%E2%80%9311_Toyota_vehicle_ recalls; www.cicpmc.org/en/detail.asp?id=3157 &Channel=2&ClassID=14*) |
| Avon Products Inc (U.S.) [Foreign-invested enterprise] | Corruption: Business bribery | May, 2011, Avon Products Inc., the world's largest direct seller of cosmetics, has found itself tangled up in allegations of bribery and deteriorating results in its China operations. On May 5, Avon announced at an annual meeting that it had fired four executives. (*Source: www.reuters.com/article/us-avon-idUSTRE7A06HC20111101; www.cicpmc. org/en/detail.asp?id=3157&Channel=2&Clas sID=14*) |

*(Continued)*

(Continued)

| Company name (country) [company type] | CSR problems | Scandal happened in China |
|---|---|---|
| GlaxoSmithKline, GSK (U.K.) [Foreign-invested enterprise] | Human rights: Damage public interests | June, 2011, British pharmaceutical GSK was ordered by Chinese authorities to recall an antibiotic used to treat infections in children, which was found to be tainted with a plasticizer, DIDP. Studies show that long-term consumption of DIDP may damage liver functions. (*Source: en.wikipedia.org/wiki/GlaxoSmithKline; www.cicpmc.org/en/detail.asp?id=3157&Chan nel=2&ClassID=14*) |
| ConocoPhillips (U.S.) [Foreign-invested enterprises] and China National Offshore Oil Corporation, CNOOC (China) [State-owned enterprise] | Environmental protection: Pollution | ConocoPhillips, the American oil company caused two oil spills in June 2011 that engulfed large swaths of Bohai Bay in North China. The two spills, involving 3,200 barrels of oil and drilling fluids, occurred in the country's largest offshore oilfield, called Penglai 19–3, and spread over at least 324 square miles in Bohai Bay. The oil field is 51% owned by CNOOC, and 49% owned by ConocoPhillips. (*Source: www.nytimes.com/2011/08/26/world/ asia/26china.html; www.cicpmc.org/en/detail. asp?id=3157&Channel=2&ClassID=14*) |
| Procter & Gamble, P&G (U.S.) [Foreign-invested enterprises] | Human rights: Damage public interests | July, 2011, Manufacturer P&G recalled two types of Oral B mouthwash in China. The products could contain a form of bacteria which is commonly found in water and soil, it poses "little medical risk to healthy people" as claimed by P&G officials. However, actually it could be dangerous for people with weakened immune systems or those suffering from chronic lung diseases. (*Source: www.pghongkong.com/en-US/News/ Detail.aspx?Id=268; www.cicpmc.org/en/detail. asp?id=3157&Channel=2&ClassID=14*) |
| Unilever (U.K/ Holland) [Foreign-invested enterprises] | Society: Disrupt market order Human rights: Damage public interests | In 2011, consumer product giant Unilever was fined by The National Development and Reform Commission for its high-profile dissemination of possible price hikes in China. In March, 2011, Unilever issued price increase notices to supermarkets in China, saying the company planned to raise the prices of some of its products. This led to panic buying and seriously disturbed regular market order. (*Source: china.org.cn/business/2011–12/19/ content_24190770.htm; www.cicpmc.org/en/ detail.asp?id=3157&Channel=2&ClassID=14*) |

| Company name (country) [company type] | CSR problems | Scandal happened in China |
|---|---|---|
| China National Offshore Oil Corporation, CNOOC (China) [State-owned enterprise] | Environmental protection: Pollution | Dec., 2011, Zhuhai Maritime Bureau received notice of undersea natural gas pipeline leak from CNOOC's gas processing terminal. CNOOC spill has occurred three times in 2011, including the serious oil spill occurred in China's largest offshore oil field Pendlai 19–3. (*Source: www.offshoreenergytoday.com/china-zhuhai-msa-reports-gas-leak-from-subsea-pipeline-cnooc-shuts-production/; www.cicpmc. org/en/detail.asp?id=3157&Channel=2&Clas sID=14*) |
| PetroChina Company Limited, PetroChina (China) [State-owned enterprise] | Environmental protection: Pollution | July, 2011, PetroChina shut down a 200,000 barrel-per-day crude distillation unit at its Dalian refinery after a fire on July 16. The accident happened just two weeks after the CDU was restarted after being shut down for around 40 days for maintenance. A similar accident happened exactly one year ago on July 16, 2010. August 29, 2011, a fire broke out at a diesel tank at PetroChina's Dalian refinery, the second fire to hit the major oil plant in less than two months. A diesel tank storing about 800 tonnes of fuel was ignited. In a short period of time, the oil company encountered two accidents and is therefore maintaining an unsafe production line, a reflection of the safety and management issues surrounding this oil company. (*Source: www.yahoo.com/news/petrochina-says-refinery-fire-dalian-put-061453182.html; www. cicpmc.org/en/detail.asp?id=3157&Channel=2 &ClassID=14*) |
| Johnson & Johnson (U.S.) [Foreign-invested enterprises] | Human rights: Damage public interests | Nov., 2011, The Campaign for Safe Cosmetics released a report saying that Johnson & Johnson still sells baby shampoo that contains chemicals harmful to babies in 13 countries, including China, while the company sells such products in at least eight other countries without the harmful chemicals. The organization has been urging Johnson & Johnson to remove two chemicals from its baby products since 2009. However, no order was made by Johnson & Johnson to recall its problem shampoo in China. (*Source: english.sina.com/ business/p/2011/1103/411280.html; www. cicpmc.org/en/detail.asp?id=3157&Channel=2 &ClassID=14*) |

(*Continued*)

(Continued)

| Company name (country) [company type] | CSR problems | Scandal happened in China |
|---|---|---|
| Siemens (Germany) [Foreign-invested enterprises] | Human rights: Damage public interests | Nov., 2011, household electrical appliance industry exposed the quality problem of Siemens' product. Consumers complain that Siemens refrigerator door does not close tightly. However, Siemens' explanation says, they are responsible for person, in comply with safety standards at the same time let the premise of air tightness accords with a requirement, Siemens door doesn't close tight is not a problem, but " want to securing the door" problem. Because historically some children were locked in the refrigerator. "Not closed too tight" can ensure the door can be pushed from the inside. (*Source: hk.crntt.com/ doc/1019/1/3/9/101913956.html?coluid=73&k indid=7151&docid=101913956; www.cicpmc. org/en/detail.asp?id=3157&Channel=2&Clas sID=14*) |
| China Grain Reserves Corporation (China) [State-owned enterprise] | Corruption: Business bribery | Dec., 2011, the former head and party secretary of the administration is being held and investigated on suspicion of corruption according to shuanggui (雙規), an extra-legal form of detention used on members of the Chinese Communist Party. There have been many other instances of corruption in the Henan grain industry ahead of this latest scandal. One of the most serious and shocking cases is the corruption of Wang Yongcheng, the former head of Grain Administration in the city of Zhoukou. Wang was sentenced to 18 years in prison in 2009 after being found guilty of accepting bribes of over 1.38 million yuan. That case caused a large stir in the grain industry across the country. (*Source: www.eeo.com.cn/ ens/2011/1213/217944.shtml; www.cicpmc. org/en/detail.asp?id=3157&Channel=2&Clas sID=14*) |
| China Guodian Corporation (China) [State-owned enterprise] | Environmental protection: Pollution | From March to May 2011, The State Electricity Regulatory Commission (SERC) set up working groups on energy-efficient supervision and inspection of emission reduction. SERC has punished relevant power plants for violations of the law on control of sulfur dioxide emissions, which is an important indicator of air quality. China Guodian Corporation Shuangliao and Hongyanchi companies were punished for excessive discharges of sulfur dioxide at 50% and 75%, respectively. (*Source: www.cicpmc.org/en/detail.asp?id=3157 &Channel=2&ClassID=14*) |

| Company name (country) [company type] | CSR problems | Scandal happened in China |
|---|---|---|
| China Datang Corporation, CDT (China) [State-owned enterprise] | Environmental protection: Pollution | From March to May 2011, The State Electricity Regulatory Commission set up working groups on energy-efficient supervision and inspection of emission reduction, and it has punished those power plants for violations of the law on control of sulfur dioxide emissions, which is an important indicator of air quality. China Datang Corporation was punished for excessive discharges of sulfur dioxide at 67% and for polluting the environment. (*Source: www.cicpmc.org/en/detail.asp?id=3157 &Channel=2&ClassID=14*) |
| Mengniu Dairy (China) [State-owned enterprise] | Human rights: Damage public interests | In recent years, Mengniu Dairy has been noted several times to have quality issues. December, 2011, the special checks were launched by the General Administration of Quality Supervision, Inspection and Quarantine(AQSIQ), and reported that two batches of milk products made by two separate domestic dairies, including heavyweight Mengniu Dairy Group, were found to contain high levels of the cancer-causing toxin Alflatoxin M1. The level of Aflatoxin M1 in the tainted milk was more than double the national standard. (*Source: www.cicpmc.org/en/detail.asp?id=3157 &Channel=2&ClassID=14*) |

# Appendix 2

## Summary of key mandatory and voluntary standards/guidelines on CSR reporting issues in China

| No. | Year of effective | Name of standards/ guidelines | Issued by regulatory bodies or other organization | General dDescription | Mandatory (M)/voluntary (V) |
|---|---|---|---|---|---|
| 1 | 2006 | Accounting Standards for Enterprises No. 5 – Biological Assets Accounting Standards for Enterprises No. 9 – Employee Compensation Accounting Standards for Enterprises No. 16 – Government Subsidies Accounting Standards for Enterprises No. 27 – Exploitation of Petroleum and Natural Gas | The China Accounting Standards Committee under the Ministry of Finance | Require to disclose relevant information for recognition and measurement of biological assets related to the agricultural production, employee compensation, government subsidies and exploitation of petroleum and natural gas and so on | M |
| 2 | 2006 | Shenzhen Stock Exchange Social Responsibility Instructions to Listed Companies | Shenzhen Stock Exchange | Encourage the listed companies to establish a social responsibility mechanism and prepare social responsibility reports on a regular basis | V |
| 3 | 2008 | Environmental Information Disclosure Act 2007 | The State Environmental Protection Administration of China | Require to disclose environmental information | M |

| No. | Year of effective | Name of standards/ guidelines | Issued by regulatory bodies or other organization | General dDescription | Mandatory (M)/voluntary (V) |
|---|---|---|---|---|---|
| 4 | 2008 | Guidelines on Environmental Information Disclosure by Companies Listed on the Shanghai Stock Exchange | Shanghai Stock Exchange | Require to disclose environmental information and CSR strategy in format either part of CSR report or separate report | M |
| 5 | 2008 | Notification on Issuance of the Guideline on Fulfilling Social Responsibility by Central Enterprises | The State-owned Assets Supervision and Administration Commission of the State Council (SASAC) | Require to establish CSR fulfillment mechanisms and CSR information reporting systems for Central State-owned Enterprises (CSOEs) | M |
| 6 | 2008 | Shanghai Municipal Local Standards on Corporate Social Responsibility | Shanghai Municipal Bureau of Quality and Technical Supervision | Encourage enterprises regularly to report to community and employees for addressing four moral and ethical responsibilities like equity issues, environmental issues, integrity issues, and harmonious issues | V |
| 7 | 2008 | China Sustainability Reporting Guidelines for Apparel and Textile Enterprises (CSR – GATEs) | China National Textile and Apparel Council (CNTAC) | Provide guidelines with comprehensive and quantifiable indicators to enterprises to publish CSR reports | V |

(*Continued*)

(Continued)

| No. | Year of effective | Name of standards/ guidelines | Issued by regulatory bodies or other organization | General dDescription | Mandatory (M)/voluntary (V) |
|-----|------|------|------|------|------|
| 8 | 2008 | Guidelines on Social Responsibility for Industrial Corporations and Federations | 11 national industrial federations and associations engaged in iron, steel, oil, chemicals, light industry, textiles, building materials, non-ferrous metals, electric power, and mining industries. | Encourage all industrial companies and industrial federations of China to establish a CSR system with CSR reporting and performance indicators | V |
| 9 | 2008 | China Sustainability Reporting Verification Rules and Instructions (CSR – VRAI) | China National Textile and Apparel Council | Provide the measuring principles and verification procedure for the quality of the CSR reports of the textile and apparel enterprises | V |
| 10 | 2009 | Guidelines on Corporate Social Responsibility for Banking Financial Institutions in China | China Banking Industry Association (CBIA) | Advise all banks to produce a CSR report in addressing economic, social, and environmental responsibilities and submit to CBA on annual basis | V |
| 11 | 2009 | Requirement for State-Owned Enterprises to issue a CSR report within three years | The State-owned Assets Supervision and Administration Commission of the State Council (SASAC) | SASAC encourage all SOEs to issue CSR report within three years | V |
| 12 | 2009 | China's Corporate Social Responsibility Reporting Guidelines, Version 1.0 | Chinese Academy of Social Sciences (CASS) | Provide instructions and performance indicators to guide different industries to report CSR issues in China | V |

| No. | Year of effective | Name of standards/ guidelines | Issued by regulatory bodies or other organization | General dDescription | Mandatory (M)/voluntary (V) |
|---|---|---|---|---|---|
| 13 | 2010 | Management Measures for Insurance Information Disclosure | China Insurance Regulatory Commission | The Measures require that the insurance company should disclosure the basic information of the company, the accounting information, risk control situation, insurance products, solvency information and major events, etc. | M |
| 14 | 2010 | Identification Rules on Administrative Responsibility for Violation of Information Disclosure (Draft for comments) | China Securities Regulatory Commission | Enforce the transparency of information disclosure of listed companies | M |
| 15 | 2011 | China's Corporate Social Responsibility Reporting Guidelines, Version 2.0 | Chinese Academy of Social Sciences (CASS) | Provide instructions and performance indicators to guide different industries to report CSR issues in China | V |

Note: 1–10 are quoted from Noronha et al. (2013); 11–15 are quoted from Guan et al.(2013)

# Appendix 3
## GRI framework

|  | Principle | Definition |
| --- | --- | --- |
| Reporting Principles for Defining CONTENT | Materiality | The information in a report should cover topics and indicators that reflect the organization's significant economic, environmental, and social impacts, or that would substantively influence the assessments and decisions of stakeholders. |
|  | Stakeholder inclusiveness | The reporting organization should identify its stakeholders and explain in the report how it has responded to their reasonable expectations and interests. |
|  | Sustainability context | The report should present the organization's performance in the wider context of sustainability. |
|  | Completeness | Coverage of the material topics and indicators and definition of the report boundary should be sufficient to reflect significant economic, environmental, and social impacts and enable stakeholders to assess the reporting organization's performance in the reporting period. |
| Reporting Principles for Defining QUALITY | Balance | The report should reflect positive and negative aspects of the organization's performance to enable a reasoned assessment of overall performance. |
|  | Comparability | Issues and information should be selected, compiled, and reported consistently. Reported information should be presented in a manner that enables stakeholders to analyze changes in the organization's performance over time, and could support analysis relative to other organizations. |
|  | Accuracy | The reported information should be sufficiently accurate and detailed for stakeholders to assess the reporting organization's performance. |
|  | Timeliness | Reporting occurs on a regular schedule and information is available in time for stakeholders to make informed decisions. |
|  | Clarity | Information should be made available in a manner that is understandable and accessible to stakeholders using the report. |
|  | Reliability. | Information and processes used in the preparation of a report should be gathered, recorded, compiled, analyzed, and disclosed in a way that could be subject to examination and that establishes the quality and materiality of the information. |

# Appendix 4

Coverage of CSR dimensions for
largest SOEs in China from 210
annual reports and 117 social reports

| CSR dimensions | Annual report | | | | | Social report | | | | |
|---|---|---|---|---|---|---|---|---|---|---|
| | 2006 | 2007 | 2008 | 2009 | 2010 | 2006 | 2007 | 2008 | 2009 | 2010 |
| SA | 38% | 44% | 47% | 43% | 44% | 34% | 36% | 55% | 37% | 48% |
| OP | 52% | 52% | 54% | 58% | 61% | 29% | 36% | 29% | 36% | 40% |
| RP | 37% | 31% | 39% | 36% | 36% | 23% | 23% | 28% | 44% | 34% |
| GCE | 23% | 25% | 25% | 29% | 24% | 22% | 28% | 31% | 30% | 45% |
| EC | 64% | 66% | 86% | 82% | 93% | 50% | 55% | 67% | 75% | 83% |
| EN | 17% | 19% | 27% | 29% | 30% | 38% | 42% | 57% | 53% | 68% |
| LA | 29% | 37% | 43% | 45% | 46% | 43% | 65% | 84% | 72% | 77% |
| HR | 3% | 5% | 6% | 6% | 6% | 16% | 18% | 31% | 24% | 34% |
| SO | 12% | 14% | 19% | 18% | 19% | 36% | 33% | 72% | 40% | 53% |
| PR | 16% | 16% | 27% | 27% | 28% | 13% | 24% | 46% | 41% | 43% |

Note: "1" is coded in the field of a CSR aspect if relevant information is disclosed in the selected report and "0" is coded for non-disclosure. Coverage= average number of aspects covered in the report/total number of aspects required by GRI-G3.

# Appendix 5

## Statistics of content analysis results

*Annual report* columns cover **No. of words** and **Quality nature of information disclosed (average score)**. *Social report* columns cover **Quality nature of Information disclosed (Average score)**.

| Indicators | Aspects | No. of words | | | | | Quality nature of information disclosed (average score) | | | | | Quality nature of Information disclosed (Average score) | | | | |
|---|---|---|---|---|---|---|---|---|---|---|---|---|---|---|---|---|
| | | 2006 | 2007 | 2008 | 2009 | 2010 | 2006 | 2007 | 2008 | 2009 | 2010 | 2006 | 2007 | 2008 | 2009 | 2010 |
| EC | Economic performance | 45,231 | 47,678 | 62,157 | 59,256 | 67,292 | 4.8 | 4.6 | 5.0 | 5.0 | 5.0 | 3.8 | 3.9 | 4.1 | 3.4 | 4.5 |
| | Market presence | 403 | 718 | 536 | 512 | 598 | 3.4 | 3.7 | 4.7 | 4.2 | 4.9 | 2.4 | 1.9 | 1.6 | 1.7 | 1.4 |
| | Indirect economic impacts | 3,597 | 2,290 | 2,547 | 1,008 | 3,423 | 2.1 | 2.6 | 3.3 | 3.1 | 2.9 | 1.8 | 1.6 | 1.3 | 1.2 | 1.7 |
| | **Average** | | | | | | **3.43** | **3.63** | **4.33** | **4.10** | **4.27** | **2.67** | **2.47** | **2.33** | **2.10** | **2.53** |
| | **Subtotal** | **49,231** | **50,686** | **65,240** | **60,776** | **71,313** | **10.3** | **10.9** | **13.0** | **12.3** | **12.8** | **8.0** | **7.4** | **7.0** | **6.3** | **7.6** |
| EN | Materials | 116 | 124 | 364 | 235 | 345 | 1.2 | 1.6 | 3.8 | 3.4 | 3.7 | 1.3 | 2.8 | 3.8 | 3.7 | 4.2 |
| | Energy | 112 | 288 | 423 | 312 | 234 | 2.4 | 2.8 | 2.6 | 2.8 | 2.6 | – | 1.2 | 3.4 | 4.2 | 3.5 |
| | Water | 123 | 456 | 513 | 751 | 643 | 1.6 | 2.6 | 3.1 | 3.7 | 3.4 | 2.6 | – | 3.6 | 3.3 | 3.7 |
| | Biodiversity | 156 | 87 | 146 | 196 | 282 | 1.4 | 1.6 | 2.6 | 2.2 | 2.8 | – | – | 1.6 | 1.3 | 1.2 |
| | Emissions, effluents and waste | 31 | 56 | 215 | 264 | 124 | 1.8 | 2.6 | 4.0 | 4.3 | 4.2 | – | – | 4.1 | 4.2 | 4.1 |
| | Products and services | 58 | 345 | 618 | 652 | 578 | 1.2 | 1.2 | 1.6 | 1.2 | 1.4 | 2.6 | 3.7 | 3.5 | 3.6 | 3.3 |
| | Compliance | 7 | 6 | 13 | – | 2 | 1.2 | 1.2 | 1.8 | – | 1.6 | – | – | 1.4 | 2.8 | 3.0 |
| | Transport | – | – | – | – | – | – | – | – | – | – | – | 2.4 | 1.2 | 3.0 | 2.4 |
| | Overall | 2 | – | 5 | – | 2 | 1.0 | – | 1.2 | – | 3.0 | 1.3 | 1.1 | 1.6 | 1.8 | 3.4 |
| | **Average** | | | | | | **1.31** | **1.51** | **2.30** | **1.96** | **2.52** | **0.87** | **1.24** | **2.69** | **3.10** | **3.20** |
| | **Subtotal** | **605** | **1,362** | **2,297** | **2,410** | **2,210** | **11.8** | **13.6** | **20.7** | **17.6** | **22.7** | **7.8** | **11.2** | **24.2** | **27.9** | **28.8** |
| LA | Employment | 2,228 | 2,475 | 2,443 | 2,156 | 2,778 | 3.6 | 3.2 | 3.3 | 3.2 | 3.6 | 4.1 | 3.3 | 4.1 | 3.8 | 3.6 |
| | Labor/management relations | – | | | | | | | | | | 3.0 | 1.6 | – | 1.7 | 1.2 |
| | Occupational health and | 2,109 | 3,171 | 3,547 | 3,672 | 3,216 | 3.4 | 3.4 | 3.7 | 3.7 | 3.4 | – | 3.6 | 4.1 | 3.6 | 3.6 |

| | | | | | | | | | | | | | | | | |
|---|---|---|---|---|---|---|---|---|---|---|---|---|---|---|---|---|
| | Training and education | 401 | 518 | 995 | 465 | 843 | 2.3 | 2.8 | 2.4 | 2.2 | 2.6 | 2.2 | 2.4 | 2.3 | 2.6 | 2.2 |
| | Diversity and equal opportunity | 43 | 110 | 115 | 138 | 216 | 1.3 | 1.4 | 1.2 | 1.6 | 1.4 | 1.5 | – | 1.0 | 1.2 | 1.0 |
| **Average** | | | | | | | **2.12** | **2.16** | **2.12** | **2.14** | **2.20** | **2.16** | **2.18** | **2.30** | **2.58** | **2.32** |
| **Subtotal** | | **4,781** | **6,274** | **7,100** | **6,431** | **7,053** | **10.6** | **10.8** | **10.6** | **10.7** | **11.0** | **10.8** | **10.9** | **11.5** | **12.9** | **11.6** |
| **HR** | Investment and procurement practices | 2 | – | 2 | 1 | – | 1.5 | – | 1.0 | 1.0 | – | – | – | 1.6 | 3.2 | 1.6 |
| | Non-discrimination | – | – | – | – | – | – | – | – | – | – | – | – | – | 2.0 | – |
| | Freedom of association and collective bargaining | – | – | – | – | – | – | – | – | – | – | – | – | – | – | – |
| | Child labor | – | – | – | – | – | – | – | – | – | – | – | – | – | – | – |
| | Forced and compulsory labor | 40 | 34 | 78 | 63 | 85 | 1.0 | 1.0 | 1.0 | 1.2 | 1.0 | – | – | 2.6 | 2.2 | 1.2 |
| | Security practices | 25 | 79 | 152 | 127 | 176 | 1.2 | 1.6 | 1.0 | 1.8 | 1.3 | 1.4 | – | 2.6 | 1.3 | 2.2 |
| | Indigenous rights | – | – | – | – | – | – | – | – | – | – | – | – | 1.6 | – | 1.3 |
| **Average** | | | | | | | **0.53** | **0.37** | **0.43** | **0.57** | **0.33** | **0.20** | – | **1.20** | **1.24** | **0.90** |
| **Subtotal** | | **67** | **113** | **232** | **191** | **261** | **3.7** | **2.6** | **3.0** | **4.0** | **2.3** | **1.4** | – | **8.4** | **8.7** | **6.3** |
| **SO** | Community | 10 | 386 | 345 | 659 | 547 | 1.2 | 1.6 | 1.5 | 1.2 | 1.3 | 2.4 | 2.2 | 2.8 | 3.4 | 2.4 |
| | Corruption | 2 | – | 6 | 1 | 1 | 4.5 | – | 3.2 | 4.0 | 4.0 | – | – | – | – | – |
| | Public policy | 590 | 639 | 832 | 791 | 636 | 2.3 | 2.2 | 3.8 | 3.4 | 3.6 | 1.2 | 3.4 | 2.8 | 3.5 | 3.8 |
| | Anti-com-petitive behavior | – | 6 | – | 3 | 2 | – | 1.3 | – | 2.0 | 1.8 | – | – | – | – | 1.2 |
| | Compliance | 266 | 291 | 1,471 | 1,645 | 1,498 | 1.1 | 1.4 | 1.2 | 1.4 | 1.2 | 1.8 | 3.4 | 4.2 | 4.6 | 4.7 |
| **Average** | | | | | | | **1.82** | **1.30** | **1.94** | **2.40** | **2.38** | **1.08** | **1.80** | **1.96** | **2.30** | **2.42** |
| **Subtotal** | | **868** | **1,322** | **2,654** | **3,099** | **2,684** | **9.1** | **6.5** | **9.7** | **12.0** | **11.9** | **5.4** | **9.0** | **9.8** | **11.5** | **12.1** |
| **PR** | Customer health and safety | 194 | 487 | 520 | 587 | 429 | 2.0 | 1.4 | 3.2 | 2.8 | 3.3 | 1.2 | 3.6 | 4.1 | 4.3 | 4.6 |
| | Product and service labeling | 446 | 788 | 829 | 725 | 1,067 | 2.4 | 2.6 | 2.4 | 2.1 | 2.8 | 2.0 | 1.2 | 3.4 | 1.6 | 3.8 |
| | Marketing communications | 412 | 235 | 297 | 354 | 128 | 2.6 | 2.8 | 3.1 | 2.4 | 3.5 | – | – | 1.2 | – | 3.2 |
| | Customer privacy | – | – | – | – | – | – | – | – | – | – | – | – | – | – | 2.0 |
| | Compliance | 268 | 965 | 568 | 673 | 924 | 1.4 | 1.2 | 1.7 | 1.6 | 1.4 | 2.6 | 3.3 | 3.3 | 3.6 | 3.4 |
| **Average** | | | | | | | **1.68** | **1.60** | **2.08** | **1.78** | **2.20** | **1.16** | **1.62** | **2.40** | **1.90** | **3.40** |
| **Subtotal** | | **1,320** | **2,475** | **2,214** | **2,339** | **2,548** | **8.4** | **8.0** | **10.4** | **8.9** | **11.0** | **5.8** | **8.1** | **12.0** | **9.5** | **17.0** |
| **Total** | | **56,872** | **62,232** | **79,737** | **75,246** | **86,069** | **53.9** | **52.4** | **67.4** | **65.5** | **71.7** | **39.2** | **46.6** | **72.9** | **76.8** | **83.4** |
| | | | | | | **Average score** | **1.59** | **1.54** | **1.98** | **1.93** | **2.11** | **1.15** | **1.37** | **2.14** | **2.26** | **2.45** |

# Appendix 6
## Disclosure of bad news and industrial accidents

| Industry category | Industry name | Bad news and industrial accidents reported | | Mass media exposure |
|---|---|---|---|---|
| | | Annual report (2006–2010) | Social report (2006–2010) | |
| A | Agriculture, forestry, livestock farming and fishery | 3 | 0 | >6 |
| B | Mining | 18 | 23 | >63 |
| C-1 | Manufacturing (light) | 9 | 7 | >12 |
| C-2 | Manufacturing (heavy) | 7 | 16 | >23 |
| D | Electric power, gas, water production and supply | 1 | 3 | >4 |
| E | Construction | 2 | 1 | >1 |
| F | Transport and storage | 0 | 1 | >2 |
| G | Information Technology | 1 | 0 | >1 |
| H | Wholesale and retail trade | 0 | 2 | >4 |
| I | Finance and insurance | 1 | 2 | >2 |
| J | Real estate | 2 | 3 | >6 |
| K | Social service | 0 | 0 | >7 |
| L | Communication and Cultural Industry | 0 | 0 | >2 |
| M | Comprehensive | 1 | 0 | >3 |
| | Total | 49 | 58 | 132 |

# Appendix 7

## Ranking of CSR reporting by industries

| | Score | | | | | | Ranking | | | | | |
|---|---|---|---|---|---|---|---|---|---|---|---|---|
| | 2006 | 2007 | 2008 | 2009 | 2010 | Total | 2006 | 2007 | 2008 | 2009 | 2010 | 5-year |
| B | 63.1 | 83.7 | 91.9 | 96 | 87.9 | 422.6 | 1 | 1 | 1 | 1 | 1 | 1 |
| I | 59.1 | 72.3 | 90.7 | 76.7 | 78 | 376.8 | 2 | 2 | 2 | 2 | 2 | 2 |
| D | 47.9 | 52.1 | 72.1 | 56 | 64.2 | 292.3 | 7 | 3 | 3 | 6 | 3 | 3 |
| C2 | 49.4 | 47.9 | 52.3 | 61.1 | 54.6 | 265.3 | 5 | 5 | 5 | 5 | 7 | 4 |
| C1 | 52.5 | 43.9 | 48 | 67.7 | 49.7 | 261.8 | 4 | 8 | 9 | 3 | 10 | 5 |
| G | 54.6 | 47.8 | 48.6 | 44.8 | 58 | 253.8 | 3 | 6 | 7 | 10 | 4 | 6 |
| F | 36.5 | 45.7 | 54.5 | 61.5 | 50.5 | 248.7 | 12 | 7 | 4 | 4 | 9 | 7 |
| E | 43.8 | 50 | 48.4 | 48.3 | 55 | 245.5 | 9 | 4 | 8 | 7 | 6 | 8 |
| J | 48.6 | 43.7 | 45.5 | 39.7 | 55.1 | 232.6 | 6 | 9 | 10 | 13 | 5 | 9 |
| L | 45.4 | 39.7 | 38.5 | 45.2 | 51.5 | 220.3 | 8 | 11 | 12 | 9 | 8 | 10 |
| M | 40.4 | 42.4 | 44.4 | 41.3 | 42.2 | 210.7 | 10 | 10 | 11 | 12 | 11 | 11 |
| A | 40.2 | 34.6 | 36.8 | 44.5 | 42.1 | 198.2 | 11 | 12 | 13 | 11 | 12 | 12 |
| K | 35.4 | 33.1 | 50.8 | 48 | 30.4 | 197.7 | 13 | 14 | 6 | 8 | 14 | 13 |
| H | 31.4 | 33.8 | 31.8 | 37 | 36.8 | 170.8 | 14 | 13 | 14 | 14 | 13 | 14 |

# Appendix 8

## Statistics on foreign direct investments

| Year | Actually utilized value (in USD 100,000,000) (in a hundred million USD) | SFEJV% | CFCE% | WFOE% |
|------|-------------------------------------------------------------------------|--------|-------|-------|
| 1985 | 19.56   | 32.0  | 55.2  | 0.7  |
| 1986 | 22.44   | 48.5  | 47.9  | 0.7  |
| 1987 | 23.14   | 52.6  | 34.6  | 12.7 |
| 1988 | 31.94   | 59.2  | 30.8  | 9.0  |
| 1989 | 33.92   | 47.9  | 19.3  | 29.5 |
| 1990 | 34.87   | 40.1  | 19.0  | 2.9  |
| 1991 | 43.66   | 50.8  | 17.8  | 30.6 |
| 1992 | 110.08  | 50.1  | 22.8  | 27.0 |
| 1993 | 275.15  | 49.5  | 22.3  | 27.3 |
| 1994 | 337.67  | 48.6  | 24.6  | 26.5 |
| 1995 | 375.21  | 43.5  | 19.5  | 36.9 |
| 1996 | 417.26  | 43.5  | 19.5  | 36.9 |
| 1997 | 452.57  | 40.6  | 23.7  | 34.6 |
| 1998 | 454.63  | 33.2  | 22.4  | 41.8 |
| 1999 | 403.19  | 32.8  | 16.2  | 50.2 |
| 2000 | 407.15  | 32.0  | 12.8  | 54.3 |
| 2001 | 468.78  | 25.34 | 12.0  | 62.1 |
| 2002 | 527.43  | 22.35 | 7.51  | 69.1 |
| 2003 | 535.05  | 22.17 | 6.5   | 70.9 |
| 2004 | 606.30  | 18.00 | 5.07  | 76.4 |
| 2005 | 603.25  | 17.20 | 4.6   | 77.2 |
| 2006 | 630.21  | 17.0  | 4.2   | 78.2 |
| 2007 | 747.68  | 20.9  | 1.9   | 76.6 |
| 2008 | 923.95  | 18.7  | 2.1   | 78.3 |
| 2009 | 900.33  | 19.2  | 2.2   | 76.3 |
| 2010 | 1057.35 | 21.3  | 1.5   | 76.6 |
| 2011 | 1160.11 | 18.5  | 15.1  | 78.6 |
| 2012 | 1117.16 | 19.4  | 2.1   | 77.1 |
| 2013 | 1175.86 | 20.2  | 1.7   | 76.2 |
| 2014 | 1195.62 | 17.6  | 1.4   | 79.1 |
| 2015 | 1262.67 | 20.5  | 1.5   | 75.5 |

(Source: China Statistical Year Book, 1985–2015, available at www.stats.gov.cn/)

Note: SFEJV denotes Sino-foreign equity joint venture; CFCE denotes Chinese-foreign cooperative enterprises; WFOE denotes wholly foreign-owned enterprises.

# Index

Page numbers in italic indicate a figure and page numbers in bold indicate a table on the corresponding page.

administrative and governance system in China 20–22
Ahlstrom, D. 105
All-China Federation of Industry and Commerce 64
all-round development stage of SOEs 31–32
Annan, Kofi 17

Barnett, M. 3
Belal, A. 2, 10, 16
*Blue Book of Corporate Social Responsibility* 11
bottom-up model of CSR reporting 100–101, *102–103*
bourgeois political economy (BPE) 13
Brammer, S. 90
Bruton, G. D. 105
Bureau of Scientific Research of the Chinese Academy of Social Sciences 11

capital nature of Chinese private enterprises 52–53
China: administrative and governance system in 20–22; corporate scandals in 2–3; legal norms with CSR ingredients 22, **23–24**; legislation on stakeholders 24–28; as world's second largest economy 2; *see also* CSR (corporate social responsibility) reporting, China
China Accounting Standards Committee (CASC) 32
China Banking Industry Association (CBIA) 33, 46
China Banking Regulatory Commission (CBRC) 46

China Datang Corporation 2
China Federation of Industrial Economics (CFIE) 46
China International Council for the Promotion of Multinational Corporations (CICPMC) 2
China National Petroleum Corporation 42
China National Textile and Apparel Council (CNTAC) 32–33, 46
China Securities Regulatory Commission 7
China Securities Regulatory Commission (CSRC) 34
*China WTO Tribune* 3
Chinese Academy of International Trade and Economic Cooperation (CAITEC) 79, 83
Chinese Communist Party (CCP) 4, 52, 54, 100
Chinese People's Political Consultative Conference (CPPCC) 88
classical political economy (CPE) 13
community and media informational pressures on CSR reporting framework 105
consumer protection laws 26
content analysis 6–7; based on GRI 34–37; results 37–42
creditors 24–25, 55–56
CSR (corporate social responsibility) reporting: general background on 1–2; research problem and objectives 4–5; specific background on 2–3
CSR (corporate social responsibility) reporting, China: administrative and governance systems and 20–22;

association relation and 88; bottom-up model of 100–101, *102–103*; framework of private and multinational enterprises 103–105; in high-profile and low-profile industries 44–47; impacts on foreign investment 74–78; legal norms 22, **23–24**; legislation on stakeholders and 24–28; literature review 10–11; media attention and 89; multilayered framework for 98–106; by multinational companies 79–86, 103–105; political relation and 88; of private enterprises 61–66; research contributions 8; research design 5, 6; research methodology 6–8; research problem and objectives 4–5; specific background in China 2–3; of state-owned enterprises 30–43, 88–89, 98–106; theoretical framework 12–15; top-down model of 98–100; triangulation in analysis of 87–97; *see also* social accounting and reporting (SAR)

Deegan, C. 14, 101
Deephouse, D. L. 103–104
Deng Xiaoping 51–52
descriptive statistics 90–91
development period in foreign investment 73–74
Dierkes, M. 15

economic performance indicators 17
employee/labor laws 25–26, 57, 82–83
energy consumption by private enterprises 56–57
environmental performance indicators 17
environmental provisions *versus* government subsidies 49
equity incentive schemes 48–49
exploration stage in foreign investment 71–72

foreign-investment in China: CSR impacts of 74–78; CSR reporting framework of 103–105; CSR reporting quantity and quality 81–85; development period 73–74; evolution process 71–74; exploration stage 71–72; introduction to 70–71; overview of CSR reporting and 79–81; reporting incentives 85; transition period in 72–73
Foxconn 2

general background on CSR reporting 1–2
Global Reporting Initiative (GRI) 17, 34–37, 106
Gray, R. 1, 16
GRI *see* Global Reporting Initiative (GRI)
Guangcai program 55

Hubbard, G. 16
Hu Jintao 4, 64, 100
human rights: and labor protection by private enterprises 57; performance indicators 18

industrial and institutional forces on CSR reporting framework 104–105
Institute of Social and Ethical Accountability 18
international SAR initiatives 16–18
interviews, research 7–8, 93–96

Jiang Wei 51
Jones, M. J. 16

Kramer, M. R. 88
Kuo, L. 40

labor laws 25–26, 57, 82–83
labor practices and decent work performance indicators 18
legal norms with CSR ingredients 22, **23–24**
legislation on stakeholders 24–28
legitimacy theory (LT) 12, *13*, 14, 101, 106
Lewis, L. 14
Li, H. B. 87
literature review, SAR 10–11

Mackey, A. 3
market players 27
Marx, Karl 13
Mengniu Dairy 2
Momin, M. 10
multinational companies (MNC) *see* foreign-investment in China

National People's Congress (NPC) 88
Neumann, W. 34

Pavelin, S. 90
political economy theory (PET) 13, 101, 106
pollution by private enterprises 56–57

Porter, M. E. 88
Preston, L. 15
private enterprises, Chinese: capital
  nature of 52–53; conclusion on 59;
  CSR disclosure on websites 66, 67;
  CSR reporting framework of 103–105;
  CSR reporting practices of 61–66; CSR
  weakness of 66–68; existing problems
  with 55–59; government forces on
  62–64; high energy consumption and
  serious pollution 56–57; historical
  background of 51–52; introduction
  to 51; lack of credit 55–56; overseas
  expansion need 65–66; poor production
  environment 58–59; social role
  of 53–55; tax evasion and lack of
  charitable activities by 57–58; weak
  social security in 59
production environment in private
  enterprises 58–59
product responsibility performance
  indicators 18

recycling technology 57
regression analysis 7, 91–93
regulatory bodies 32–34, 104
Responsible Competitiveness
  Framework 18

San Lu Corporation 2–3
SAR *see* social accounting and reporting
  (SAR)
Shenzhen Stock Exchange (SZSE) 32
Shuanghui Group 2–3
social accounting and reporting (SAR)
  1, 5; content analysis and 7, 34–42;
  development of 15–16; international
  initiatives 16–18; interviews 7–8,
  93–96; model 16; regression analysis
  7, 91–93; research approach 18–19;
  research design 5, 6; researches in
  Western and Chinese academia
  10–11; theoretical framework 12–15;
  triangulation in analysis of 87–97
social function stage of SOEs 30–31
social role of Chinese private enterprises
  53–55
social security, weak 59
society and community protection laws
  26–27
society performance indicators 18
SOEs *see* state-owned enterprises (SOEs)

specific background on CSR reporting 2–3
stakeholders, legislation on 24–28
stakeholder theory (ST) 12, *13*,
  14–15, 101
State Council of the PRC (SCPRC) 22
State Environmental Protection
  Administration (SEPA) 32
State Grid Corporation of China (SGCC)
  12
State-owned Assets Supervision and
  Administration Commission (SASAC)
  32–33, 35, 43, 48
state-owned enterprises (SOEs):
  conclusion on 42–43; content analysis
  based on GRI 34–37; content analysis
  results 37–42; CSR reporting in
  high-profile and low-profile industries
  44–47; environmental provisions
  *versus* government subsidies for 49;
  equity incentive scheme for high-level
  management in 48–49; introduction
  to 30; multilayered CSR reporting
  framework of 98–106; other findings
  based on qualitative analysis of CSR
  reports from 47–49; pressures from
  government and regulatory bodies
  32–34; stages of development 30–34;
  taxes on 47–48; triangulation and CSR
  reporting by 88–89
subsidies, government 49
systems-oriented theories 12

taxation 47–48; evasion and lack of
  charitable activities 57–58
top-down model of CSR reporting 98–100
transition period in foreign investment
  72–73
triangulation: empirical study 87–93;
  introduction to 87

Unerman, J. 14
UN Global Compact 17
univariate analysis 91

value retaining and increment stage of
  SOEs 31

Williams, S. 13
World Trade Organization (WTO)
  52, 73

Zijin Mining Group 42

For Product Safety Concerns and Information please contact our EU
representative  GPSR@taylorandfrancis.com
Taylor & Francis Verlag GmbH, Kaufingerstraße 24, 80331 München, Germany

www.ingramcontent.com/pod-product-compliance
Ingram Content Group UK Ltd.
Pitfield, Milton Keynes, MK11 3LW, UK
UKHW020946180425
457613UK00019B/555